Co-education Reconsidered

OPEN UNIVERSITY PRESS
Gender and Education Series

Editors

ROSEMARY DEEM

Lecturer in the School of Education at the Open University

GABY WEINER

Course Manager in the School of Education at the Open University

The series provides compact and clear accounts of relevant research and practice in the field of gender and education. It is aimed at trainee and practising teachers, and parents and others with an educational interest in ending gender inequality. All age-ranges will be included, and there will be an emphasis on ethnicity as well as gender. Series authors are all established educational practitioners or researchers.

TITLES IN THE SERIES

Co-education Reconsidered
Rosemary Deem (ed.)

Just a Bunch of Girls
Gaby Weiner (ed.)

In preparation
Women and Adult Education
Sallie Westwood

Women and Training
Ann Wickham

Co-education Reconsidered

Edited by
ROSEMARY DEEM

OPEN UNIVERSITY PRESS

Milton Keynes · Philadelphia

Open University Press
Open University Educational Enterprises Limited
12 Cofferidge Close
Stony Stratford
Milton Keynes MK11 1BY, England
and
242 Cherry Street
Philadelphia, PA 19106, USA

First published 1984
Reprinted 1987

British Library Cataloguing in Publication Data
Co-education reconsidered.
1. Co-education
I. Deem, Rosemary
371.2'52   LC1601

ISBN 0–335–10417–7

Text design by Clark Williams
Cover design by Phil Atkins

Typesetting by S & S Press, Abingdon, Oxfordshire
Printed in Great Britain by
Thomson Litho Ltd, East Kilbride, Scotland

CONTENTS

Until recently, expressions of concern about issues of girls' under-representation and experience of discrimination in schooling have been limited to feminist academics, and, in a few instances, groups of committed teachers.

This series, aimed at non-feminists as well as feminists, pupils, parents and teachers as well as academics, incorporates work by practitioners who have developed their own analyses and strategies for dealing with sexism in schools. Their record of experience will, it is hoped, contribute to the development of a non-discriminatory pedagogy that will also take into account racism and other forms of bias within education.

This book, the first in the series, displays the most important characteristics of the series. It looks at co- education as a gender issue and, raising practical issues as well as historical and theoretical perspectives, treats co-education as problematic, presenting arguments and justifications for and against its continued existence.

The first three chapters (by Brehoney, Shaw & Arnot) discuss the historical and theoretical implications of mixed and single-sex schooling for both girls and boys, and show how, increasingly during the twentieth century, co-education has come to be regarded as 'a good thing' despite evidence that it is likely to academically disadvantage girls.

The final two chapters focus on the ways in which teachers in mixed schools have sought to address some of the most explicit forms of gender-inequality in education. In the first case this is by the formation of a working party to review whole school policy and practice (Stantonbury Campus Sexism in Education Group) and in the second, by separating girls and boys for certain subjects (Smith).

Within this book (and within the series) two distinct approaches in dealing with gender bias or discrimination in education can be discerned. The first advocates increased equality of opportunity for *all* pupils, regarding the expansion of opportunity as dependent on improved teaching methods and strategies. Whilst it recognizes that many girls are likely to come off worst at school, it argues that this can be dealt with by improvement in practice rather than by girls gaining at the expense of boys.

An alternative view sees equality of opportunity within narrower confines. Gender inequalities within education are seen as part of the wider social pattern of inequalities between the sexes, with men in the dominant positions. Here it is held that advances by girls and women in education will only be made if boys and men stand down and either voluntarily or compulsorily give up their 'hold' on the education system.

This book shows that advocates of single-sex schools are likely to hold the second view and supporters of mixed schools, the first.

Gaby Weiner

ACKNOWLEDGEMENTS

I should like to thank John Skelton of Open University Press for all his encouragement and help with this volume. Earlier versions of my ideas on co-education were given as papers to the University of York Department of Education part-time MA course in 1981 and to the DES Regional Course on 'Teaching Girls in secondary schools' at IM Marsh Campus, Liverpool Polytechnic in 1982. Particular thanks are due to Jenny Shaw, who was interested in co-education long before my own interest developed, and to colleagues and postgraduate students (especially Gaby Weiner and Sheila Scraton) in the School of Education, the Open University, with whom I have often discussed the issues surrounding sexism in schools.

Rosemary Deem is a Lecturer in the School of Education, the Open University, Opposition Labour Group Spokesperson on Education on Buckinghamshire County Council, and a governor of Bridgewater Hall School, Stantonbury Campus.

Kevin Brehony is a Lecturer in Education at Edgehill College of Higher Education, Ormskirk and is currently researching the history of progressivism in education in England and Wales.

Jennifer Shaw is a Lecturer in Sociology at the University of Sussex and has been researching the issues surrounding co-education for several years.

Madeleine Arnot is a Lecturer in the School of Education, the Open University, and has been writing for several years about women and education.

Stantonbury Campus Sexism in Education Group comprises a number of teachers (mainly from Bridgewater Hall School) at Stantonbury Campus, Milton Keynes, Bucks.

Stuart Smith is a former Deputy Head of Stamford High School, Tameside, and is currently researching single-sex setting with the aid of an EOC grant.

ABBREVIATIONS

APU   Assessment of Performance Unit
CSE   Certificate of Secondary Education
DES   Department of Education and Science
EOC   Equal Opportunities Commission
GCE   General Certificate of Education
HMI   Her Majesty's Inspectors [of schools]
ILEA   Inner London Education Authority
LEA   Local Education Authority
MSC   Manpower Services Commission
NFER   National Foundation for Educational Research
NUT   National Union of Teachers
OU   The Open University
TESA   Teacher Expectation and Student Achievement
       programme

Co-education Reconsidered — Reviving the Debate

ROSEMARY DEEM

Eighteen months ago I remember mentioning to a friend that I was starting to put together a book about co-education and single-sex schools. Before I had time to explain what the book might concern itself with, my friend exclaimed 'Oh . . . I hope you're not going to end up advocating those dreadful single-sex schools are you? . . . awful places . . . I went to one myself . . . it took me years afterwards to adjust . . . I couldn't relate to men at all when I left school'. Her reaction is not an untypical one; many people believe that there is no room for debate about the merits of co-education; that it *must* be better than single-sex schooling. And indeed, as Weinberg[1] has noted there has been very little debate or discussion about co-education in the period since 1944, despite the fact that many single-sex secondary schools in the state sector have disappeared since then. Such schools are retained to a greater extent in the private sector, but even some of these are exploring such possibilities as mixed sixth forms.[2] Why, then, revive the issue? Well, there are several reasons why. Firstly, a number of reports and studies over the past ten years have raised the matter of whether co-education at the secondary school stage necessarily offers equal educational opportunities to both sexes, especially with regard to option choices in the later years of schooling and in relation to classroom management of boys and girls by their teachers.[3] Secondly, the remaining single-sex schools in the state sector are dwindling in numbers, and soon it may be too late to learn anything from their existence or experiences. Thirdly, with the coming of age of comprehensive schools, critiques and appraisals of such schools have started to appear[4] and amongst the questions which can be asked about comprehensives is whether they have served children of both sexes equally well, both socially and academically.

The intention of this short collection is to reconsider the concerns and issues surrounding co-education at the secondary school stage during the twentieth century, in practice as well as in theory, beginning with the early part of the century, and moving right up to the present day. By so doing we hope that some of those with an interest in education (teachers, parents, governors) who, perhaps, have never even given the question of 'co-education or not?' a single thought, will begin to think through the implications of co-educating girls and boys, and perhaps consider whether this practice is working. It is important to say at the outset that we write from a variety of perspectives and positions, and that there is no single set of policy recommendations that we would wish to make collectively. We are not wholeheartedly advocating a return to all single-sex schools, nor suggesting that co-education can only work if we adopt single-sex setting, although both of these are implied in some of the arguments advanced here. Furthermore, we are not unaware of the current problems surrounding state education, from cuts in public expenditure, through falling rolls, to high unemployment rates for young people. It would be extremely optimistic to expect that issues concerning inequalities in the schooling of girls and boys would necessarily take priority, at a time when the entire educational scene in Britain is under pressure from a variety of sources and groups. Additionally, we recognize that gender divisions are cross-cut by other divisions such as class and ethnicity. Nevertheless it is essential that we recognize the right of both sexes to an equal education (and equal does not necessarily mean 'the same', because in a society whose very structure, practices and beliefs are heavily marked by socially constructed gender division, the sexes do not stand equal on admission to secondary school, and offering both girls and boys the *same* opportunities and facilities cannot lead to equality of opportunity, still less equality of outcome). This must be recognized as an important principle and starting point for good practice by everyone with an interest in education, whether parents, classroom teachers, headteachers or policy-makers. By drawing to people's attention the extent to which the ideals of co-education and the realities of mixed schooling differ we can waymark one path to understanding why gender inequalities persist in education, despite growing awareness of the problem, the existence of sex discrimination legislation and the efforts of the Equal Opportunities Commission (EOC).[5]

In Chapter 1, Kevin Brehony looks at some of the origins of ideas about co-education in the early part of the twentieth century, noting that co-education can be distinguished, ideologically at any rate, from mixed schooling. Brehony observes that the debate surrounding co-education in the early decades of the twentieth century was concerned with the social (rather than academic or cognitive) implications of male–female power relations, and with the perceived need to remove conventional constraints on freedom (for instance, so-called 'artificial' sex differences). The major proponents of co-education were often middle-class progressives whose world views contained more than a tinge of 'alternative' culture and romanticism. Co-education, as defined by Alice Woods in 1919 meant that both sexes were taught most subjects in common, without sex-segregation.[6] This was distinguished from mere mixed schooling already in existence during the nineteenth century in both state and private sectors (sometimes for reasons of cheapness) which segregated girls from boys socially and academically within the same buildings. The private sector of education, notably schools like Bedales and the King Alfred schools formed a vanguard for the development of co-education in Woods' sense of the term, stressing the social advantages of co-educating the sexes. These included, for example, the reduction of homosexuality amongst boys; less rough behaviour from boys subjected to the civilizing influence of girls; the replication of relationships within the family and adult world; it was argued that co-educating would help produce healthier marriages, and a wider choice of occupations for both sexes, and it could offer a great range of educational experiences to girls and boys. Co-education had its critics, including those who feared it would encourage sexual promiscuity.

For instance, the Association of Headmistresses, as well as the feminists, thought that the curriculum of co-educational schools would be unsuited to girls, and that the interests of girls would be sacrificed for those of boys. These critics also foresaw the gradual disappearance of women headteachers if co-education were universally adopted. It is interesting that the concerns of these two latter groups are in many respects identical to those voiced by contemporary critics of co-education.[7] Brehony points out that Inspectors' Reports on some leading private co-educational schools found them either to be boys' schools which admitted girls, or primarily girls' schools in which there were few boys aged over 13 years. There was frequently a predominance of male staff, craft subjects were segregated by sex, and there was little evidence available on the relative attainments of girls and boys. Brehony concludes that the case for co-education put in the early twentieth century was a fragile one, based on romanticism, individualism and personal strategies rather than social solutions to girls' lack of equal opportunities. Further, co-educationalists lacked any recognition of the deep-rooted nature of male dominance over women in society generally, such that schooling might not be able to provide an answer, and the cognitive outcomes or implications of co-education were largely ignored.

Jennifer Shaw sets out a carefully constructed argument about the contemporary politics of advocating single-sex schools in Chapter 2. It is ironic that the groups of progressives to whom Brehony's chapter refers advocated co-education for exactly the reasons some feminists now favour single-sex schools — that these establishments offer a solution to sex differences in education. Shaw notes that arguments against retaining single-sex schools include the lack of evidence in their favour. For example, recently Bone in a study carried out for the EOC has concluded that neither type of school favours gender equalities,[8] and the 1982 ILEA report on all its secondary schools says single-sex schools make little difference to academic achievement for girls.[9] Other reasons against single-sex schooling are the supposed lesser importance of gender as opposed to class in the debate about equal opportunities (see Lodge and Blackstone, 1982; Rubenstein, 1979) and the view that given time, gender inequalities will disappear of their own accord. Shaw points out the lack of discussion about co-education's merits in more recent decades, and the possibility that class selection under the tripartite system of education established in 1944 may be replaced by a new form of class *and* gender selection in mixed comprehensives. The latter issues have also been raised recently by other educational commentators.[10] Shaw advances the suggestion that despite the criticisms levelled at them, single-sex schools can make possible the move away from the belief that sex discrimination is the fault of individuals, by providing a basis for shared gender solidarity. She points out that gender is both a social and a structural division which cannot be solved by individualistic solutions and that failure to recognize this is one reason why few gender inequalities have so far disappeared; the interlinking of class and gender in comprehensive schools having prevented rather than encouraged any real structural change in female–male power relations. As she says, whilst education can lead to changes in class position, it cannot change someone's gender. Shaw directs attention to the fact that real parental

choice of a single-sex or mixed school is largely confined to
the private sector. She makes a similar point to Brehony in
Chapter 1, namely that co-education started out as a serious challenge to an inequalitarian system, but has failed
because it has misrecognized or ignored the importance of
both formal and informal barriers to gender equality, and
has not understood the structural significance to society of
gender divisions. Co-education only appears to be progressive; in reality it offers individual solutions to a social
and collective problem; and hence, contends Shaw, we
should instead support single-sex schools as a way of moving towards more collective and solidary solutions to gender inequalities.

Madeleine Arnot offers a rather different perspective in
Chapter 3, arguing that the real issues about equality of
gender opportunity concern not whether schools are mixed
or single-sex, but whether we are educating boys in ways
which don't necessitate them having power and privilege
over women, and which don't define masculinity as being
in sharp contrast to femininity. The problems girls face in
schooling are, in part, a problem of how boys are schooled,
says Arnot. Taking up points already made in previous
chapters (and raised subsequently in Chapter 5) about the
ways in which boys and male teachers often dominate in
mixed schools, and noting also the tendency for girls and
boys to specialize in different areas of the secondary school
curriculum, Arnot claims that ideologies about male breadwinners and dependent wives or mothers still influence
much of the schooling of both sexes. Boys are oriented
towards a life of paid work (with perhaps disastrous results
if unemployment is high) and girls are directed towards
the home and childrearing. Making a similar argument to
the one which emerges from Bone's recent re-analysis of
the statistical evidence on mixed and single-sex schools for
the EOC,[11] namely that the type of school makes little difference to gender inequalities (especially those suffered by
girls), Arnot says that what we need to find are new ways
of reducing sexism in all types of school, whether mixed or

sex-segregated. This can only be done, she contends, by developing new and more positive forms of masculinity, which do not depend on the devaluing of women and absolute polarization from femininity. But such changes need to occur outside schools in the wider society as well, because gender inequalities are deeply rooted in patriarchal and capitalist societies. Furthermore, changing ideologies about forms of masculinity involves a challenge to male power and privileges in all social classes, a point also made by Brehony and Shaw. Men as well as women need to consent to such changes, says Arnot, and one way to prepare the ground for this is to stop using gender as an organizing variable in education, and move to a completely mixed system of schooling. This also has the merit of being more economic in the use of resources than are single-sex establishments.

Chapters 4 and 5 see a shift from the historical, the theoretical and the analytic levels of the co-education debate towards a more detailed discussion of the practicalities of mixed schooling, and the possibilities for developing greater equality of educational opportunity for both sexes. In Chapter 4 a group of teachers from a 'progressive' mixed comprehensive school campus, nationally recognized for its innovatory stance on many educational issues[12] (and which has moved towards a common-core curriculum which avoids some of the worst excesses of the polarized subject option choices pointed out by Arnot in Chapter 3) outline some of the problems of sexism encountered on that campus. The group also discuss some of the strategies presently being used at Stantonbury to try to combat gender inequalities, and the remaining areas of concern. Examining in turn English, which is a subject traditionally liked by and associated with girls, maths and sciences, which are often seen as predominantly male preserves, and recreational studies (a more traditional school might call this physical education) which theoretically at least, operates mixed teaching in an area of the curriculum still heavily sex-segregated in most schools, they consider what has been done so far and the difficulties encountered. Expenditure cuts are one such difficulty, resulting, for instance, in a male-dominated staff in the Recreation Studies Faculty. The strategies employed range from careful book buying and use of sympathetic Mode III exam syllabuses in English, to 'Be a Sumbody' maths conferences for girls and integrated science courses rather than physics, chemistry and biology. The group conclude their discussion by outlining the main areas of schooling where sexism should be monitored.

In Chapter 5 Stuart Smith explores the experiments in single-sex setting conducted at Stamford High School, Tameside. The experiments were begun originally because the school consistently found itself faced with a problem of female under-achievement in mathematics, physics and chemistry. Smith notes that the evidence on whether girls attain better results in maths or sciences in single-sex schools is patchy and often conflicting, whereas an attempt to compare single-sex sets with mixed sets in a single school reduces many of the variables and allows a more controlled analysis. As Shaw, Arnot and Brehony indicate in earlier chapters, one of the most consistently emerging barriers to girls' equality of opportunity in mixed schools is the behaviour of boys, their greater degree of teacher attention, and their tendency to dominate lessons. This was found to be the case at Stamford School, especially for the few girls in the top GCE maths set in the fourth year, and seemed to have a considerable effect on their attempts to pass 'O' level maths. One of the important points Smith makes in detailing the single-sex setting strategies is that initially not every teacher involved was wholeheartedly committed to the idea; most were at least a little sceptical. Timetabling difficulties have precluded widespread use of single-sex setting throughout all years in the school, although the experiment was extended in 1980 to science as well for some year groups. Whilst the academic attainment results do not show overwhelming success for the limited experiments conducted so far, they do show some improvement in maths and science performance for girls placed in single-sex sets during at least part of their secondary school career. Furthermore, the girls concerned, whilst not wanting to revert to single-sex schools, or to single-sex setting in all subjects, have enjoyed the experience, and felt the benefits of not being taught alongside boys in subjects where they lack confidence. Smith warns that single-sex sets are not an educational panacea which will solve gender inequalities in educational attainment overnight (and clearly they will not solve problems of girls' academic performance which arise from social class or ethnic disadvantage) and points out the necessity for carefully controlled long-term research on the strategies themselves before firm conclusions can be drawn. Also, as Chapter 4 notes, single-sex setting may conflict with some schools' aim to have mixed-ability groups. Nevertheless, single-sex setting does seem to offer one way of ensuring that the so-called 'social objectives' of co-education are not achieved at the expense of girls' academic performance and cognitive development.

Just to reiterate the point made at the beginning of this introduction, we are not in this collection advocating any one single solution to the problems of gender inequalities and sexism in schools. As you read through the chapters you will find different points of view, and a variety of suggested strategies. What unites the contributors, however, is firstly a belief that gender discrimination cannot be overcome by individualistic solutions, whether these take place in single-sex or mixed schools, and secondly commitment to changing our educational system so that neither sex is disadvantaged in schools. If by writing this book we succeed in getting people, whether teachers, pupils, parents, governors or policy-makers to reconsider the issues surrounding co-education and equality of opportunity for both sexes, then we shall have achieved something very valuable.

Notes

1 See Weinberg (1981) who discusses the nature of the non-debate about co-education in the period since 1945.
2 Walford (1983) looks at these schemes to include girls in the sixth-forms of non-state boys' schools.
3 See DES (1975) and (1979), Shaw (1980), Spender (1982a) and Stevens (1983).
4 See Moon (1983) Shaw (1983) and Hargreaves (1982).
5 Wilce (1983a) looks at the history of the EOC's interventions into education.
6 Woods (1919).
7 See Spender (1982a), Shaw (1980) and Wilce's (1983b) article on the findings of the Women's National Commission on the decline in the number of women head teachers (from 25 per cent of all secondary heads in 1963 to 16 per cent in 1983).
8 Stevens (1983) gives a preliminary review of the study's findings. The study itself was still unpublished at the time of going to press.
9 ILEA (1982).
10 For instance Hargreaves (1982) and Shaw (1983).
11 Stevens (1983).
12 See Moon (1983) for a detailed discussion of the innovations carried out by Stantonbury and five other comprehensive schools over the past decade.

CHAPTER 1

Co-education: perspectives and debates in the early twentieth century

KEVIN BREHONY

The debate on mixed or single-sex schooling raises not only wider issues of women's inequality and the continued dominance of male power in our society but also the extent to which schooling can redress that imbalance. The key mechanism by which inequalities of power can be reduced through schooling has for long been seen as the wider provision of equal educational opportunities. The supporters of co-education claimed that it provided women with greater educational opportunities than single-sex schools and they laid great stress upon the school as an instrument of social change. My intention here is to examine this view critically by looking at the origins of the concept of co-education, the historical conditions in which it arose, the arguments advanced for it and its associated practices. The period examined is roughly that between 1900 and 1920 which precludes the consideration of important figures like A. S. Neil, W. B. Curry and the Russells. Nevertheless, much of the case for co-education was extremely repetitious and by the early 1920s its main features were already present.

An historical perspective on co-education has more than an antiquarian interest. Although conditions have changed considerably since the notion of co-education was first produced, the terms of the debate are still recognizable. In addition, mixed schooling has entered the common sense of teachers and others almost by stealth. The assumptions upon which, if any, its justification is based are remarkably similar to those advanced by the co-educationalists considered here. Like education as practised in today's schools co-education has assumed in some liberal circles the status of a 'good thing' which critics challenge at their peril. A critical appraisal of such a sedimented notion is long overdue.

During the nineteenth century mixed schooling in England, particularly in the working-class elementary schools, was not unexceptional but it was only during the last decades of the century that the distinctive notion of co-education began to take shape. Alice Woods, a prominent advocate of co-education who had been head of a co-educational school at Chiswick (1884–92) defined co-education as:

> the education of boys and girls . . . in companionship from the age of infancy to adult life, neither sex being segregated, but taught many subjects and sharing many games in common, with freedom to enjoy their leisure in one another's company.[1]

Such a definition was open to widely different interpretations but nevertheless in England at least, it was both novel and challenging to existing practices, particularly in the sphere of secondary education.

In contrast to the present, secondary education at the time was not defined in terms of universal provision to pupils above the age of 11 years. Many secondary schools of the private or the proprietary type received young children and taught them in preparatory or kindergarten departments. In essence, secondary education was a social category, which was often used interchangeably with the phrase, 'middle-class education'. The demand and support for co-education came overwhelmingly from a section of the class which utilized the secondary schools and consequently these schools were at the centre of the debate.

It is important to specify more clearly who the supporters

and propagandists for co-education were. Noticeably, the leaders of the movement were nearly all men.[2] In 1923 the Report of the Consultative Committee on the Differentiation of the Curriculum for Boys and Girls Respectively in Secondary Schools, noted that while co-education was advocated by some of its men witnesses only two women witnesses favoured it.[3] Secondly, arguments for co-education arose from within a cultural milieu which may be termed 'alternative'. In the eyes of the public in general this middle class-alternative culture was associated with crankiness, sandals, fresh air and vegetarianism. Thus, as one writer put it: 'Co-education had against it at the outset all those forces which tend to keep society stable'.[4]

This pressure for co-education was not an isolated one but formed part of a general demand of middle-class 'progressives' for the breaking down of barriers to individual self-development and liberty of expression. These objectives were closely linked to older romantic and democratic traditions stressing equality of opportunity. In this attack on convention and the prejudices of the past a key task was the exposure of constraints to freedom and opportunity as social constructions. However, while it is evident that supporters of co-education believed that single-sex schooling was based upon artificially constructed 'sex-differences' (in order to deny equality of educational opportunity to women), their presentation of their case was tentative. As in the following formulation, their argument was frequently presented in terms of a scientific experiment:

> until we have exposed both sexes to similar conditions we cannot tell what differences are inherent and unalterable, and what merely the resultants of a different upbringing.[5]

The emergence of co-education as an issue at the turn of the century may only be explained in part by the erosion of Victorian certainties. A second powerful determinant was the slow but perceptible growth of mixed secondary schools during the last decade of the nineteenth century. Concern about how these schools should be organized provided an opportunity for the co-educationalists to intervene. But first their extent and their practices had to be discovered. In November 1901, in a response to a request from Alice Woods, Margaret Close Shipman provided the names of eight secondary schools in England which she held to be co-educational. By the following January, Shipman had produced twelve more.[6] This exploratory work enabled Woods, in 1903, to produce a list of twenty-nine co-educational schools.

These lists are curious because of the schools that were omitted. The long tradition of mixed schooling in Scotland was ignored. The tradition of mixed secondary schooling in Lancashire which Sheila Fletcher has referred to,[7] was registered only by the appearance of the names of three Lancashire schools on Shipman's original list of eight. In Wales, where since the Welsh Intermediate Education Act of 1889 seven mixed secondary schools had been established by local authorities,[8] there had developed a body of experience which was also barely mentioned in the growing progressive, literature on co-education. Neither would readers of the lists of schools gather that there were, in 1897, thirty-one mixed endowed grammar schools in England. The inference may reasonably be drawn that these omissions, together with those of the elementary schools (of which in England in 1902, 65 per cent were 'co-educational')[9] were part of a conscious effort to distinguish co-education from what existed in mixed schools. Such schools were not mixed on social or educational grounds but (particularly in areas of low population density) for reasons of economy. A review of the situation in Wales makes this abundantly clear. Faced with the problem of securing secondary school places for girls, the organizers of Welsh schooling adopted a programme of the establishment of 'dual' and 'mixed' schools. In the 'dual' schools, boys and girls were educated separately. Mixed schools in which boys and girls were taught together, were established initially only 'in thinly populated districts'. The 'dual schools', however, were seen as an 'acceptable compromise' as they provided:

for the education of girls on a cheaper plan than that of separate schools, and it introduced the experiment of co-education with the maximum of cautiousness.[10]

If the economic attraction of mixed schooling had been overwhelming and universal then it might have been expected that mixed schools would have rapidly become the norm in the years following the Act of 1902. This Act established local authorities to provide secondary schools. However, ranged against those persuaded by the need for financial stringency were women teachers in girls' schools, and a much larger body of opinion, fearful of the possible erosion of control over pupils' sexuality and fearful that boys would become effeminate.

What occurred therefore, in the years immediately following the 1902 Education Act, was a growth in absolute terms in the number of mixed schools on the Board of Education's Secondary grant list from 184 in 1904–5 to 331 by 1921–22.[11] But much of this growth may be attributed to the higher grade or higher elementary schools which became municipal secondary schools under the control of the new local authorities.[12] These schools were an outgrowth of the elementary school system which, as has been observed, had a high proportion of mixed schools. However, this growth in mixed schools of just over 44 per cent needs to be set alongside a 78 per cent increase in girls' secondary schools during the same period. Moreover, by 1921–2, as a proportion of all schools on the grant list, the share of mixed schools was falling. In that year they constituted about a quarter of all schools. If the schools not included on the grant list are added then the proportion of mixed schools was even less.

While the gradual development of mixed schools in the state sector provided the conditions for a debate on the merits of co-education, the progressive supporters of co-education concentrated their efforts mainly in the private schools. Two main reasons were put forward for this strategy; firstly, it was argued that only boarding schools could provide the necessary family atmosphere and secondly, they were free from 'tradition, charters, or Government red tape' to experiment.[13] In the private sector, the schools run by the Society of Friends had been mixed for a long period but only at the turn of the century did some of them become co-educational.[14] In contrast, most of the 'New Schools', which formed an important wing of the progressive education movement, were co-educational from the outset. Indeed, by 1921, the International Bureau for New Schools included co-education as a key distinguishing characteristic of these New Schools.[15]

Ironically, the head of the first of these New Schools, Cecil Reddie—who opened Abbotsholme in Derbyshire in 1889—was a misogynist and a strong opponent of co-education.[16] In 1893, J. H. Badley, one of first members of staff to be appointed at Abbotsholme, left to found Bedales School, which moved to Petersfield in Hampshire in 1900. Five years after its establishment, as a result of pressure from Badley's wife (who supported the suffragettes) Bedales admitted girls.[17] In the same year, 1898, the Rev Cecil Grant opened Keswick School in Cumberland which was, from the outset, co-educational. Also in 1898, the King Alfred School Society opened a co-educational school in Hampstead. Its first head, Charles E. Rice had previously taught at Bedales—but before it had become co-educational. Other co-educational schools which followed were St George's, Harpenden to which the Rev Cecil Grant moved in 1907, the Home School at Grindleford in Derbyshire opened by Susan Platt (a former HMI) and her husband in 1910 and the schools begun in Letchworth by Theosophists. Of these St Christophers, opened in 1920, is perhaps the best known.

Another group of private schools which were mixed—but not strictly co-educational by Woods' criteria, as boys tended to leave them at an early age—were those associated with the Froebel movement. Among these were Lady Barn School near Manchester, opened in 1873 by William Herford (a prominent supporter of Froebel's ideas), and the Froebel Educational Institute in London begun in

1895. The Froebelian contribution to the cause of co-education was, however, less one of the founding of experimental schools and more one of propaganda. The most assiduous of the Froebelian propagandists for co-education was Alice Woods.[18]

The progressive private schools, because of their freedom to innovate and because of their status derived from their predominantly middle-class intake (which was determined by their relatively high fees) rapidly achieved an influence and reputation disproportionate to their number and size. Within a short period Badley, Grant and Woods projected themselves as experts on co-education and were constituted as such by semi-state bodies. Woods appeared before the Royal Commission on Secondary Education (Bryce) in 1894 and was questioned on co-education, on the basis of her work at Chiswick.[19] Articles on co-education by Badley and Grant appeared in the volumes of the Board of Education's 'intelligence unit', the office of Special Reports and Inquiries.[20] Badley and Grant also had articles on co-education published in 1908 in the report of an international investigation into moral instruction.[21] The report was edited by Michael Sadler, formerly director of the office of Special Reports and Inquiries who was sympathetic to the cause of co-education. In this way a semi-official ideology of co-education was constructed largely by default. The Board of Education and the local authorities drew on the experiences of the co-educational schools but the subject was never exposed to an official investigation and the Board's policy remained decidely ambivalent towards it.

The ideological justifications produced for co-education by the progressives were frequently contradictory and incoherent. However, this may be seen as a strength rather than as a limitation as the ideology was able to link together many widely differing interests. Two examples will suffice. Along with Badley, Alice Woods was the most tireless propagandist for co-education. In addition to editing two collections of articles on co-education in 1903 and

1919, Woods produced an avalanche of articles for journals arguing her case. In an autobiographical section of a book written in 1920, she recounted how as a child, she experienced an intense longing for the liberty enjoyed by boys,[22] for 'work and action' and for access to education. In her view, co-education was primarily a strategy for widening girls' educational and occupational opportunities.

A very different emphasis appears in the arguments of the Rev Cecil Grant, for him co-education was desirable because of the advantages it held for boys. His central preoccupation was with what he termed the 'immorality' prevalent in public schools. In 1903, several years before Alex Waugh's *Loom of Youth* initiated a widespread debate on homosexuality in public schools, Grant contended that: 'immorality in schools is a disease, coming and going in epidemics of varying violence.'[23] In his view, co-education was likely to produce a 'weakening of the temptation towards impurity'.[24] Grant and his supporters were so concerned with the 'moral health' of boys that in order to counter the argument that co-education might lead to sexual relations between boys and girls, Alfred Perks, a teacher at Grant's Keswick School, maintained that even if this 'evil' occurred, it would be 'less disastrous' than the 'moral ill-health' existing in single-sex schools.[25]

Two other major lines of division are discernible in the arguments and practices of the co-educationalists. Firstly, there were those like Grant who assumed the existence of 'sexual differences' not only at the physical level but also at the level of interests and personality. Caroline Herford, on the other hand, denied the relevance to education of differences other than physical. Secondly, a division occurred over the age at which co-education was felt to be appropriate. The main issue involved here concerned the perceived necessity to prepare pupils for the sexual division of labour from 13 or 14 years of age. Many co-educational schools ceased to retain boys at this age as their parents removed them to single-sex schools in order to prepare them for examinations and a future career. Sadler agreed and argued that the educational needs of boys and girls began to diverge at this age as girls required an education which prepared them for homemaking and motherhood.[26] The Platts, in contrast, maintained that: 'the co-education girl is a marrying girl and makes a good wife'.[27]

Despite this diversity and inconsistency it is still possible to identify positions which were held in common by most of the supporters of co-education. What united Grant and Woods, for example, was a stress on the hoped for social outcomes of co-education and a corresponding lack of attention to what may be termed its cognitive outcomes. This was because the key to the construction of a better future for progressives generally lay in an education which respected and fostered individuality. But first, individual differences had to be discovered and identified by providing equality of opportunity. Once differences had been revealed (ran Badley's argument for example) a decision had then to be made as to whether or not they provided grounds for separate educational treatment. That decision in turn was largely determined by the progressives' educational aim, which for Badley was the production of 'a complete human being'.[28] Given this objective, girls' (or boys') academic achievement was of less importance than the contribution which co-education could make to the attainment of social goals. At this point the claims asserted for the co-educational elixir became extravagant. For example Homer Lane (the founder of the Little Commonwealth, a self-governing institution for delinquents), wrote that co-education:

> will not only free human society from that intolerance which makes for destruction and hatred, but also will enable the individual to perceive truth through which goodness can be developed and a sense of beauty acquired.[29]

From these flights of fancy the descent is steep to the modest hope of the 'idiot teacher', E. F. O'Neill that social reforms would follow if 'boys are familiar with the problems of cooking, sewing and baby care'.[30]

Of all the social outcomes predicted for co-education the one most frequently mentioned was hinted at in phrases like the 'perfection of the relations between man and woman'.[31] This has a double connotation. In one usage it referred to 'sex warfare' and its resolution, behind which lay the struggle for the enfranchisement of women and the conflicts it gave rise to. This was joined in the 1920s by a middle-class sexual revolution which challenged the old certainties upholding the parameters of sexual behaviour and led to a growing concern among progressive educators with the regulation of sexuality. This concern lay behind Badley's view that co-education combatted 'silliness or worse' by postponing the emergence of 'sex-conscious-ness' and it allowed 'the natural sex-attraction to develop on sounder lines of comradeship'.[32] In this approach, Bad-ley was supported by Kenneth Richmond who provided the legitimacy of a 'psycho-analyst's view'[33] and by John Russell, the head of King Alfred School, who stated that co-education would make 'a sordid marriage' less likely.

The appeal by Badley to what was natural constituted a second common, though contradictory, strand in the argu-ment and was linked very closely to a veneration of the family and its adoption as the model which progressive schools sought to emulate. This linkage is common enough in progressive educational thought and it was easily mobilized as an argument for co-education. Examples are numerous and Caroline Herford's statement is typical:

> . . . the teaching of boys and girls together is the natural plan, following the lead of the family.[34]

Reliance on naturalism as an argument for co-education had its dangers for this was the same ground on which many opponents of co-education argued for the separate schooling of boys and girls. Their argument was the fam-iliar one of biological determination. This was summarized by Woods as holding that 'physical differences in sex bring about differences of mental and moral characteristics' which in turn sustained a 'natural' sexual division of labour. On occasions, Woods rejected 'natural' explanations in favour of 'nurturist' or environmental ones. Men dominated the movement for reform in education, she argued, because women bore the stamp of imperfect education and 'of generations of repression and of isolation'.[35] Co-education she thought, would reveal 'the true spheres and work of each sex' by stripping away conventional and customary prejudices.

The 'natural' was rejected in favour of nurture when it suited the co-educationalists case. For Badley, girls on their own were more sensitive and emotional than boys whereas boys possessed 'strength of purpose, fearlessness, uprightness and independence'. Sidney Wells, who wrote an account of an experiment in co-education at the Battersea Polytechnic Day School for the Board of Education's Special Reports, recorded, how these 'essential' attributes were altered by co-education.

> Girls lose many little personal vanities and their tendency to titter and giggle, they acquire more vigour, energy, and self reliance, they learn to speak out and speak up and to be less self-conscious.

Boys, on the other hand become:

> more sympathetic and regardful of others feelings to be less rough in deed and coarse in word, and to be more tidy.[36]

The 'natural' order could be overturned by co-education but the overwhelming image conveyed was one of rough boys being civilized by sensitive girls. While girls were held to gain from co-education by becoming more assertive the balance of advantage lay clearly with boys.

On this point and that of the family model the co-educationalists were vulnerable to attack from women teachers in girls' schools. The Association of Headmistresses debated the issue of co-education at its conference in 1905. At the Conference, Miss Benger of Swansea County School argued that the curriculum of co-educational schools was 'unlikely to be the best for girls'. It was good for boys but girls suffered as girls were not prepared to ask questions when boys were present.[37] The suffragist, head of the North London Collegiate School, Sophie Bryant defended single-sex schooling for girls over 10 years old on the ground that: 'growing girls work in a different manner and at a different pace compared with boys' and she warned of girls in mixed schools thinking themselves to be intellectually inferior to boys as they lacked confidence which only girls schools could provide.[38]

Similar objections were raised by another suffragist, Maude Royden, in 1919. In co-educational schools, she claimed, girls were apt to resign 'initiative and leadership to boys' and that in such schools 'the interests of the girls are sacrified too much to the interests of boys'. While the co-educationalists also argued that girls gained in self-confidence when educated with boys, Royden referred to her experience in the struggle for women's suffrage which she claimed gave women: 'a sense of confidence in themselves and their powers which could hardly have been achieved otherwise'.[39]

Maude Royden also raised another issue which had been debated at the Association of Headmistresses Conference, that of headships of mixed schools. The family model adopted by the supporters of co-education required that the staff of co-educational schools be mixed and this was seen to have positive advantages. However, they were not unaware that by attempting to reproduce the conditions of family life they were also reproducing an unequal division of labour. Alice Woods saw this as only a temporary problem as perfect equality of opportunity for headships was bound to come with the growth in mutual understanding between men and women who had been educated together as children. In the meantime, she argued, 'women must be prepared to sacrifice their own interests in the advance of the common good'.[40] However the optimism of Woods did not satisfy her critics in the Association of Headmistresses who were able to point out that in 1923 there were only three women heads of mixed schools on the Board of Education's grant list.[41]

Another issue raised by Royden was that of unequal pay for equal work in co-educational schools. While Mansford, the head of a mixed grammar school at Bakewell, argued for equal pay[42] Badley justified the granting of larger salaries to men on the grounds that they had families to support. He also felt it 'natural' that men became heads of schools in preference to women as the care of her own children was a woman's prime responsibility. On the general claims of the heads of single-sex schools to provide a better education for girls, he responded by denouncing such schools as nunneries, the feminine form of the co-educationalists favourite term of abuse for boys' schools.[43]   As well as exposing some rather traditional attitudes held by Badley, this debate also highlighted the reckless optimism inherent in the case for co-education. Undoubtedly this is partly explained by the nature of the ideological conflict in which the co-educationalists were engaged. As one writer put it, their main opponents were the 'classic shades of Dr Arnold' (the boys public school tradition) and 'the familiar domestic presence of Mrs Grundy'.[44] At the same time the co-educationalists consistently misrecognized the structural determinants of the problem. At the Association of Headmistresses Conference in 1930, Dorothy Brock recounted her experiences on the Prime Minister's Committee on the Classics of 1918 which was composed of eighteen men and two women. 'At intervals', she recalled, the Committee, 'changed the word "boys" in the report to "pupils" ' and the committee 'made the most valiant efforts to remember that girls existed and to imagine what they might be like'.[45] At the heart of the matter lay what J. J. Findlay, one of England's first Professors of Education, called 'rivalry for *power in general*' between men and women.[46] Which was of course what the co-educationalists hoped to resolve but through education, whereas—as Findlay pointed out—women's equality with men had first to be achieved in all areas of social life before inequalities in education could be reduced.

Having examined some of the arguments for co-education I want now to look at the practices of those schools held up as exemplars of co-education by their founders and supporters. The purpose here is to look closely at how far the practices adopted corresponded to the rhetoric of co-education and what, if any, were the discernible outcomes. Confronted with a wide range of schools which varied as to the proportion of girls and boys admitted, whether they were day or boarding schools and the age at which the pupils left, it is not possible to draw other than general conclusions. Another confusing factor—the flexibility of the use of the term 'co-education'—is evident in the account given of the Battersea Polytechnic Day School by Wells. However, it was not one of the schools popularized by Alice Woods, and Wells soon became disaffected with co-education as he found that the 'traces of moral corruption' in co-educational schools were 'worse between boy and girl than between boy and boy'.[47]

The school contained 100 boys and thirty-nine girls and the policy adopted was to 'make as little difference as possible in the treatment of the boys and girls'. In practice, this objective allowed the holding of separate assemblies, separate drill and separate practical work, such as manual training for boys and domestic economy for girls. In addition boys and girls were not allowed to sit together nor work together in those practical classes that were mixed. Interactions between boys and girls were subject to 'constant watchfulness'. Nevertheless, Wells claimed that everything was done to 'break down all false barriers between the sexes, and to promote co-education in the fullest sense of the word'.[48]

On several counts the Battersea Polytechnic Day School failed to satisfy Alice Woods' criteria of a co-educational school but Bedales and other private schools might reasonably have been expected to approximate more closely to the co-educational ideal. Bedales occupies a special place in the construction of the case for co-education. In 1923 Badley claimed that it was the first school to apply the principle throughout the whole range of the school years. An alternative, more measured, view is provided by the reports of the HMI. This source also provides an official view of co-education in general although not, it should be stressed, the only one and certainly not the one for public consumption as the circulation of these reports was restricted and sections of them were seen only by officials of the Board of Education.

In their report for 1902 the inspectors stated that Bedales, which contained ninety-one boys and fifteen girls was not a 'mixed school' but 'more of a boys school where girls are admitted'.[49] In 1911 they criticized the inadequate accommodation for girls and women teachers and added that: 'both in numbers and ability the mistresses are overweighted by the Masters; this is in some ways disadvantageous to the girls'.[50] By 1927 the numbers of girls and boys were more or less equal but on the regular staff there were seventeen men but only nine women.

Another school which, due to the efforts of its head C. E. Rice and his successor, John Russell, was well known for its practice of co-education was that of the King Alfred Society in Hampstead. In 1903 Rice referred disapprovingly to the practice of parents removing the older boys from the school.[51] When the school was inspected in 1913 the numbers of boys and girls was almost equal but all except two of the boys were under thirteen. Thus the inspectors concluded that 'there is some danger lest it may become a girls' school to which a few boys are admitted'.[52] At St Christophers, the school opened by Theosophists in Letchworth, the inspection of 1920 found eighty-six girls and sixty-eight boys (both day and boarding pupils).[53]

This evidence demonstrates that the experiments in co-education upon which much stress was laid were, in fact, carried out in far from favourable conditions according to the standards which the co-educationalists themselves had established. Even so, three areas of school practice may be distinguished in which the co-educationalists claimed to have made significant advances. These are the content of the curriculum, punishment and physical education. There is little evidence on the first of these areas and given the stress on the social and moral aspects of schooling this is hardly surprising. However, differences in attainment between boys and girls were noted. Susan and William Platt, for example, wrote that girls 'tend to show superiority in languages, literature and history; the boys in mathematics, science and geography'.[54]

For them, however, such differences were seen not as a problem but led to 'mutual understanding'. Similarly, Cecil Grant found these differences insufficient to matter. Badley noted that girls and boys matured at different rates and that when boys began to develop rapidly in adolescence, girls needed protection from 'overstrain'. At that point greater subject choice and opportunities for separate work were introduced.[55] This differentiation of subject matter was based upon what Badley termed 'a principle of equality in difference'.

Where the curriculum was differentiated, it was mainly in those 'traditional' areas which bore some connection to pupils' expected future roles. Thus at Ladybarn School no subjects were considered more suitable for girls than for boys but girls were given additional plain sewing.[56] At Bedales and—more surprisingly because of its public school traditions—Keswick, carpentry and sewing were taken by both boys and girls. At Bedales, from which several boys became officers in the forces, a sergeant taught boys drill, fencing, boxing, riding and musketry.[57] The pattern, then, was far from uniform but if there is a shortage of evidence in the area of the formal curriculum there is even less for the 'hidden curriculum'.

The dominance of men on the staff of these schools has already been referred to, to which may be added the tendency for women to teach the younger children. It is not known whether the consequences of these imbalances were regarded as problematic. Evidence from other areas of school life suggest that they probably were not. For example at Keswick, girls were encouraged to place fresh flowers in the classrooms.[58] Discipline and punishment was another sphere in which differences were made. This figured more largely in those schools which were peripheral to the core co-educational schools like Bedales and King Alfred's where sanctions were kept to a minimum. At Battersea, for example, the punishment of girls was rare as they resolved that they would behave better than boys.[59] Boys at Keswick were subject to detention and corporal punishment whereas girls who transgressed faced detention and suspension.

Varying policies were adopted in the co-educational schools to games and physical education. This area was one which caused the inspectorate to express most unease about co-education. Alternatively, mixed games and physical education were regarded by many co-educationalists as a test of the seriousness of their committment to the cause. The inspectors' objections were rarely made explicit but the schools of the King Alfred Society were subject to their censure on this point. The approach adopted by C. E. Rice was more radical than that of Badley. At King Alfred's football was not encouraged as the girls could not play on Saturdays. The school games were hockey in winter and cricket in summer. At Bedales, in its earliest period, boys (but not girls) played football whereas boys could play hockey alongside girls. Later, the older boys played football and the girls lacrosse.[60]

In 1922 on their visit to the King Alfred Society School at Hendon, the HMI found games taught in the preparatory department in mixed classes by two masters. This arrangement, they considered, increased 'the possibility of over-strain'.[61] On the other hand, when it was found in 1928 that boys and girls in the Senior Department were taught physical education together by a woman the inspectors thought this 'radically unsound'.[62] At St Christophers, Letchworth the inspectors raised the issue of mixed physical education with the school governors. The desirability of separating boys and girls above 10 years old was stressed and it was pointed out that this was the practice at Bedales. The governors replied, 'Oh, but we are in advance of Bedales in this respect'.[63]

The co-educationalists often claimed that it was the pupils themselves who chose separate games. But none were prepared to follow Rice and abandon boys football. The greater physical strength of boys, it was argued, justified separate treatment and so girls were excluded. For Homer Lane exclusion did not mean that girls could not participate, 'footer' was a game he said 'which the female watched with enjoyment and enthusiasm and intense partisanship, without the desire, based upon sex envy, to participate'.[64] The central issue here is that of how far such practices dissolved contemporary gender stereotypes; in Lane's case they were not even regarded as a problem.

As far as the outcomes of these practices is concerned it is difficult to disentangle them from the inflated claims made by the co-educationalists themselves. Two sets of outcomes are, in principle, distinguishable: the cognitive and the social. Of course the former at some point may translate into the latter as academic success is, for a few, a route to greater social equality, but even that is not guaranteed. Contrary to the 'scientific' spirit in which the experiments were carried out no record of cognitive outcomes was ever presented. As these were viewed as unimportant for both girls and boys, the girls schools, in all probability, offered a greater chance of access to higher education to girls because they were integrated into an examination system designed for boys.

One observer referring to social outcomes found that pupils from co-educational schools had 'no self-consciousness in their relations with people of another age, or sex, or class',[65] but added that this may have been due in part to the type of parents who sent their children to such schools.

This historical account sheds little light on whether girls achieve more in mixed than in single-sex schools. Additionally the social effects of the different forms of schooling defy quantification as schools in this respect are only one set of institutions which are responsible for the production of gender relations. What does emerge is the fragility of the case for co-education and the need to treat the claims of the early co-educationalists with a great deal of scepticism. A central theme which is implicit throughout is the familiar opposition between social and personal strategies for the achievement of an end to women's oppression. The co-educationalists favoured the latter and by ignoring the social determinations reproduced, whether intentionally or not, many of the features of male domination which they sought to alleviate.

Notes

1 Woods (1919), p. 26.
2 Woods (1920), p. 25.
3 Board of Education (1923), p. 155.
4 Wedgwood (1919), p. 54.
5 Badley (1903), p. 2.
6 *Journal of Education* (1902), p. 42.
7 See Fletcher (1982), p. 95.
8 Charity Commissioners (1898), p. 51.
9 Hughes (1902), p. 348.
10 Charity Commissioners (1898), p. 10.
11 Board of Education (1923), p. 42.
12 Board of Education (1926), pp. 26–7.
13 Anon. (1913), p. 700.
14 Stewart (1968), p. 45.
15 Ferriers (1921).
16 Gathorne-Hardy (1977), p. 282.
17 *Ibid.* p. 287, but see also Bremner (1901), p. 238.
18 See variously Woods (1904a), (1904b), (1906), (1925) and (1931).
19 Royal Commission on Secondary Education (1895), pp. 1–21.
20 Badley (1900)and also Grant (1902).
21 Badley (1908).
22 Woods (1920), p. 14.
23 Grant (1902), p. 27.
24 *Ibid* p. 97.
25 Perks (1903), in Woods (1903), p. 43.
26 Sadler (1903), p. xiv.
27 Platt and Platt (1919), in Woods (1919) p. 49.

28 Badley (1900), p. 501.
29 Lane (1919), in Woods (1919) p. ix.
30 O'Neill (1919), in Woods (1919), p. 95.
31 Russell (1920), p. 357.
32 Badley (1923), p. 59–60.
33 Richmond (1919), in Woods (1919).
34 Herford (1903), p. 60–61.
35 Woods (1903), p. 113.
36 Wells (1897), p. 204.
37 Anon. (1905), p. 470 and also Price and Glenday (1975), pp. 69–70.
38 Quoted by Brock (1930), p. 19.
39 Royden (1919), in Woods (1919), p. 5.
40 Woods (1903), p. 134.
41 Board of Education (1923), p. 154.
42 Mansford (1903), in Woods (1903), p. 99–100.
43 Badley (1919), in Woods (1919).
44 Wedgwood (1919), p. 53.
45 Brock (1930).
46 Findlay (1927), p. 149.
47 *Journal of Education* (1904), p. 170.
48 Wells (1897), p. 203.
49 Public Records Office (1902), *ED109, 1863*.
50 Public Records Office (1911), *ED109, 1864*.
51 Rice (1903), in Woods (1903), p. 86.
52 Public Records Office (1913), *ED109, 3782*.
53 Public Records Office (1920), *ED109, 2102*.
54 Platt and Platt (1919), in Woods (1919), p. 40.
55 Badley (1919), pp. 21–2.
56 Herford (1903), in Woods (1903), p. 53.
57 Public Records Office (1911), *ED109, 1864*.
58 Perks (1903), in Woods, (1903), p. 40.
59 Wells (1897), p. 204.
60 Badley (1919), pp. 20–1.
61 Public Records Office (1922), *ED109, 4232*.
62 Public Records Office, *ED109, 4233*.
63 Public Records Office, *ED109, 2102*.
64 Wedgwood (1919), p. 59.

CHAPTER 2

The politics of single-sex schools

JENNIFER SHAW

There are no public institutions for the education of women, and there is accordingly nothing absurd, or fantastical, in the common course of their education. They are taught what their parents or guardian judge it necessary or useful for them to learn, and they are taught nothing else. Every part of their education tends evidently to some useful purpose: either to improve the nature and attractions of their person, or to form their mind to reserve modesty, to chastity, and to economy: to render them both more likely to become mistresses of a family and to behave properly when they have become such. In every part of her life a woman feels some conveniency or advantage from every part of her education. It seldom happens that a man, in any part of his life, derives conveniency or advantage from some of the most laborious and troublesome parts of his life.

Adam Smith, *The Wealth of Nations*, 1776

It is his role in promoting individualism as much as his ideas on education that earn Adam Smith a place at the head of this chapter. While not approving of his general sentiments, like him, I want to recommend a particular form of girls education more widely and suggest general sociological and political grounds for doing so.

Through their association with boarding, repressed sexuality and esoteric or 'classical' education, single-sex schools are counted among the peculiarities of the English education system. Most educationalists, as well as most ex-pupils, would rather that they were firmly consigned to the past and not dug up by feminists eager to appreciate all-female institutions or, worse still, recommended as a form of affirmative action. For most the cause of single-sex schools is a lost one, irretrievably reactionary and leading to unacceptable and apartheid-like proposals. Yet the issues raised are central to any understanding of inequality in education generally and, however uncomfortable, the debate should be entered. Nothing else poses so sharply the problem of the relationship between class and gender in producing educational inequalities in the first place, or more pointedly raises the question of whether formal or informal processes contribute most to their perpetuation.

There can be no doubt that the renewed interest in single-sex education is the result of feminists concerned with both identifying specific conditions which lead to sex differences in education and seeking practical solutions for them. There can also be no doubt that the whole subject sails dangerously close to prevailing right-wing winds and that feminist and educational concerns can all too easily be blown off course, or at least seem to be. In the educational context the rightwards political shift finds expression in certain interpretations of parental choice, support for selective and denominational education and the primacy given to academic over social aspects of schooling—none of which can be avoided in any discussion of single-sex or mixed schooling. In the feminist context the implication that separatism, in any form, is also anti-marxist or anti-socialist has led to some wariness in giving the topic due consideration. Thus objections to a single-sex schools counter-reformation come from a variety of sources, although they tend to follow a similar line.

In the first place it is often argued that there is no adequate data available in Great Britain on which any reasonable opinion can be based and what there is is so heavily dependent on the experience of private and grammar schools as to make generalizations virtually impossible. In part, of course, these charges are fair although the situation could easily and speedily be reversed if the DES released information from its existing returns on individual performance and presented it according to whether children were educated in single-sex or co-educational schools. A second type of objection takes a more general form, though it is related to the first through the problem of the combination of class and gender effects in educational performance. As an early commentator remarked, sexual inequality in education has never had the political pull that class has had.[1] Partly, no doubt, because while class differences are generally seen to result from social processes and therefore to be amenable to change, there is a much deeper attachment to viewing gender differences as natural and unalterable. Furthermore, what efforts have been made to deal with gender-based inequality directly (e.g. through considering the effects of single-sex or co-educational schooling) have met with the response that: (a) class remains the most pressing problem; and (b) sex differences in co-education are declining anyway. The obvious reply to the first charge is that as everyone has both a class position and a gender a concern for class that ignores gender is inadequate. It is needlessly divisive to set up class and gender as mutually exclusive foci for action, research and attention and to do so is to operate primarily as a cover for the preservation of sectoral and male interests within classes.

The second ground for according low priority to sex differences in education and to the role of single-sex or mixed schools in particular rests precariously on a mechanical and unilinear view of social change and on a faith in social trends rather than political action for changing the world that we live in. It suggests that trends are constant and may be extrapolated into the future without danger of reversal. The implication is that in time sex differences will disappear altogether. Such confidence is touching but the sociology on which it is based is less inspiring, for if the past teaches us anything it is that projections are notoriously fallible.

The re-organisation of secondary schools along comprehensive lines has been a central political fact of educational life of the post-war period but it is its byproduct, co-education, that may well be its most tangible and lasting result. In almost all education authorities comprehensive re-organization entailed a move from single-sex schooling to co-education despite the fact that there was no DES guidance or circular on the matter, no position from the Association of Education Committees and no government investigation. It is not unusual for the most enduring effects to be unintended ones but if we connive with the original disregard for the consequences of co-education we lose an opportunity to understand more about the process of social change in general and one of the most significant educational changes of this century.

Since comprehensive re-organization, over three quarters of all children—and substantially more in the state sector—are educated in mixed schools so it is a matter of some urgency that we know what the effects of each *type* of school actually are. It is clear that as a result of the comprehensive programme a certain amount of formal selection in education has been abolished. However, the conditions that lay, and still lie, behind the selection, scarcity and unequal distribution of educational resources have remained the same.[2] On theoretical grounds alone we could expect one form of selection to replace another so we should not, perhaps, be surprised if the net effect of the social changes associated with comprehensive re-organization amounted to the more obvious form of selection based on class being replaced by a form of selection based on a combination of class and gender. This operates through social processes, mainly of the interpersonal kind which flourish in the mixed setting of co-educational schools. In detailing these processes I expect to show both how sex and class interact within an educational system and demonstrate how critical single or mixed-sex schools are to the question of what constitutes equality of opportunity for girls and boys.

Before rejecting the idea of a return to single-sex schools it is worth noting Bloomfield and Pratt's[3] gloomy report to the EOC on the possibilities of secondary school re-organization. They had found the LEAs unco-operative and considered the Secretary of State more or less powerless to make the LEAs take the matter of sexual discrimination in their schools seriously. The EOC itself is constantly hampered in preparing for cases of educational discrimination by the fact that the issues are constantly posed as ones of individual victimization and thus are hard to deal with in a systematic way. What they, and we, need is an analysis that can show how it is the form of educational organization that produces discriminatory behaviour.

Thus the argument for single-sex schools is made firstly and primarily on the ground that organizations are easier to manipulate than people. Maintaining sexual divisions at the organizational level of schools can limit the scope or pattern of social evaluation and interaction which, in the context of mixed schools, culminate in sex-stereotyped curricula, sharply differentiated educational and occupational destinies and intellectual waste.

Theoretically this line of argument rests on a view of social structure whereby single-sex institutions, including schools, can provide a basis for social solidarity around a shared gender identity. Solidarity on the basis of gender is less well institutionalized than that of class and thus there are less collective resources with which the iniquities and injuries of sexual division can be resisted. Single-sex schools can provide both a model of excellence and the direct and collective experience of positive support. Where group solidarity is weak, individualism flourishes and it is the individualism characterizing education that exacerbates the pernicious effects of sexual differentiation. More pragmatically, single-sex schools as a remedy for sexual inequality in education at least has clear policy implications. If the case for them is sufficiently convincing a return to them involves no greater upheaval than that contemplated by authorities planning to dismantle their comprehensive or middle schools. The problem of falling schools rolls is, however, a serious one though the force of that argument, namely that the catchment areas for single-sex schools would be too large, was strenghtened by the decline in the school population which is now considered to be only temporary.

Early research findings certainly suggested that there was little to recommend single-sex schooling whether one took a boys or a girls interests into account. The National survey of Health and Development (1946 cohort) dealt with a period when most children were still in highly selective schooling and their results relate only to children in grammar and secondary modern schools.[4] Essentially there seemed to be no significant difference in the achievement of working-class boys and girls who went to single-sex grammar schools, but in the mixed grammar schools both working-class girls and boys had lower levels of achievement, left sooner and had lower aspirations for further education. At the time Douglas suggested an explanation in terms of initial selection. Segregated schools could choose the most able working-class children, especially girls, and once they were in the school the academic culture and intense pressure to conform would be great enough to ensure that they did well. In the secondary modern schools where the pressure was lighter the performance of working-class children of either sex was similar whether they attended single-sex or mixed schools. For middle-class children the results were somewhat different and point up the number of variables at play (class, sex and type of school) and their complex set of interactions. Middle-class girls at mixed schools reached higher educational standards than middle-class girls at single-sex schools, whereas the reverse held true for middle-class boys who were at an advantage if they attended single-sex schools. Such findings, whilst not widely publicized, were probably sufficient to quell doubts about the wisdom of going co-educational and, as Weinberg has demonstrated,[5] throughout the period when local authorities were submitting plans for secondary school re-organization the sex structure of the schools was considered a thoroughly uncontentious issue. It is only much more recently that research has begun to undermine that assumption.

The HMI's *Report on Curricular Differences in Schools* (1975) both documented the greater polarization of subject choice along sex-stereotypical lines in mixed schools and made it clear that the issue of sexual inequality between girls and boys could not continue to be discussed simply in terms of the numbers of examinations entered or passed or places gained in various types of post-secondary education.[6] This was followed by another HMI *Report on Aspects of Secondary Education in England* (1979) which showed that the curricular effects were independent of the level of provision of facilities for taking subjects.[7] In addition, in the past few years there have been a steady stream of research reports and newspaper articles which have re-examined the merits of single-sex co-educational schooling. Reports of experiments such as that conducted at Stamford school where a group of girls were taught maths in single-sex sets and showed a quite remarkable improvement have rightly attracted a lot of attention.[8]

Harding's work on sex differences in science examinations raised the discussion to a more sophisticated level by taking into account ever more complex variables.[9] Although it relates only to science, her work suggests that girls are at a disadvantage if they attend a mixed school, especially if it is a comprehensive one whereas boys do better at mixed schools. An intervening variable in her work is the type of science teaching, 'Nuffield' science or conventional methods. Whilst she found boys to be more successful than girls in mixed schools whatever type of science course they took, girls did better in all girls schools than girls in mixed schools for Nuffield biology and conventional physics. In comprehensive schools boys were generally more successful than girls in taking Nuffield chemistry and conventional physics and girls did better than boys only in those subjects if they went to single-sex schools.

The importance of all this is not simply whether it is girls or boys who do best in mixed or single-sex schools, although that is politically a crucial question, but rather that it shows first, how volatile or sensitive gender is to educational change, possibly more so than class, and second it shows how important the sex structure of a school is. We simply do not know how much of the variance between girls and boys educational performance is a result of the variance between girls and boys schools and on that depends a range of policy decisions. In the debate about school effectiveness there has been no discussion of the sex structure of schools but it is clearly important, particularly in the context of the significance given to the degree of discernible and measurable difference between types of school. As one critic has pointed out the school attended may make the difference to a child of between one and two 'O' level passes, and give them a 'competitive edge' over their less fortunate peers which he assesses as being 'roughly equivalent to the advantage that has accrued for most of the post-war period to pupils in private schools'.[10] As Gray further points out 'small' differences can be crucial, particularly in determining whether a child stays on at school or enters higher and further education. Such an approach to 'small' differences is quite unlike that usually met in the debate about sex differences in education.

Although Great Britain is not unique, the degree of sexual division in its schools has been a distinctive feature which sets its system of secondary education apart from a number of other highly developed countries where co-education is the normal pattern (e.g. the USA). As such the previously dominant pattern of single-sex education needs to be taken seriously as a *systematic* variable whose disappearance from the educational scene in Britain is both a response to and sign of major social change. If the education system is thought of as dovetailing with a labour market strongly coloured by implicit and explicit sexual divisions then a major change in schooling such as a shift into genuine co-education would constitute a major threat to the stability of the system. The change-over from single-sex schooling was in no way a response to changes in the labour market or class structure. It occurred in isolation and was primarily a matter of administrative convenience. Its isolation is just as great in the other direction having had little or no effect on the rates of female or male social mobility or degree of sexual segregation within occupations. What changes have occurred in both of these spheres are more easily explained by factors other than co-education. Female social mobility has been greater amongst those educated in the single-sex, ex-grammar sector and the pattern of occupational segregation by sex has changed direction rather than degree.[11] We should not be surprised that the introduction of co-education has been followed by a series of adjustments that have limited and contained its potential for change. Opposition to co-education, except in the private sector (where single-sex schools were defined and made an object of deliberate policy) was minimal and largely ineffective, whether voiced by ethnic groups on religious and cultural grounds or by the far-sighted few who saw that co-education might not be a costless solution to the problem of secondary school re-organization.

At a more general level the problem is that without an exceedingly firm grip on the institutions it is extremely difficult to control the redistribution of costs and benefits of any sort of deliberate institutional change, and education is replete with examples. When higher education was expanded in Great Britain following the Robbins Report the social group that 'benefited' most (i.e. increased their proportionate share of university places) was middle-class girls and not the working-class boys and girls for whom, in ideological terms, the expansion was intended.[12] At the time a concern with the 'wastage' of natural talent and 'national resources', as represented by the under-education of the working classes led to a fairly straightforward acceptance of Robbins' dramatic and sweeping proposal that higher education should be available to *all* who

wanted it and fulfilled the minimum entrance requirements. But, despite their rhetoric, neither the expansion
nor the reforms of the post-war period were truly egalitarian in class terms each suffering, as Gray has pointed
out, from the 'woolly minded' assumption that 'potentially
egalitarian reforms can be piggy-backed upon expansio-
nary ones'.[13]

A similar process has occurred in secondary education as
a result of the introduction of co-education generally,
although the mechanics are rather different, because of the
difference in the degree of formal and informal selection
used in secondary and higher education. Where formal
selection is retained, expansionist programmes like the
growth of higher education have not affected the overall
distribution of educational take-up but, more surprisingly,
neither have programmes such as co-education which, in
principle, are genuinely redistributive. Because they
occurred within the compulsory and universal sector they
produced responses at the informal level which ensured
that, by and large, the conventional distribution of benefits
are preserved. On educational grounds it was well known
that the levels of material provision and staffing in boys'
schools exceeded that of girls' schools,[14] especially in the
science subjects, and thus it seemed only reasonable and
indeed enlightened to conclude that a pooling of those
resources would lead to more equality of opportunity between the sexes. Yet we can now see that the results were
rather different and it is to a possible explanation of these
results that I now turn.

I shall do so on theoretical grounds whilst recognizing
that in the end what is most important is the careful evaluation of controlled experiments like those at Stamford
School, few and far between though they are at present.
However, more of these might be encouraged by the following arguments.

Some years ago Lockwood[15] introduced a distinction
between social integration and system integration which
not only highlighted the difference between the processes

that welded individuals into some sort of stable pattern of integration and those that bound the structural parts of the social system together but also gave insight generally into the process of social change. Although he called the distinction 'entirely artificial' and the argument was written against the backdrop of the then fierce opposition between functionalist and conflict 'theorists' it pointed up the fact that conflict could be both endemic and intense and yet not lead to structural change whilst, conversely, not all change was accompanied by overt conflict. Today it is less urgent to press for a consideration of the contradictions between the material base of a society and its institutional order, such an approach no longer being either unusual or unacceptable; however, Lockwood's categories remain useful when considering the interaction between class and gender inequality and the significance of the growth of co-educational schooling.

Just as it is important not to reduce gender and gender divisions to the interpersonal, psychological or ideological and leave class and class divisions as structural or material categories and constraints we must be careful not to similarly reduce the social/system distinction to the more familiar one of informal/formal, related though they may be. Moreover, it is necessary to illustrate with examples drawn from the educational field what might be meant by employing these categories. A lot of the controversy surrounding the discussion of sexual divisions in education centres on whether the labour market and its sub-divisions substantially affect the nature, content, direction and outcomes of schooling or whether schools are reasonably independent of it but nevertheless sexually divisive and thus in need of explanation in terms of ideology and stereotyping. In the first instance it is *system integration* that is being stressed (i.e. the relationship between the two institutional orders of education and the labour market), whereas the second type of argument rests on an analysis of forms of social integration. In his original article Lockwood further argued that the two levels or types of

integration were connected in a way that had implications
for the rate and degree of social change, 'since the only systematically differentiated parts of a society are its institutional patterns the only source of social disorder arising
from system disorder is that which takes the form of role
conflict stemming from incompatible institutional patterns'.[16] If social change will occur only if a disjunction or
contradiction arising at the structural level is accompanied
by role conflict, then presumably the converse is true too
and social change will not occur if such role conflict is
averted.

At a systematic level the integration of class and gender
within education does much to prevent serious role conflict arising. This is illustrated by the fact that single-sex
schooling has been preserved primarily within the private
sector or within that part of the state system still committed
to selective secondary education. The exemptions granted
to independent schools through the Sex Discrimination
Act demonstrate a double standard and contrast with the
process whereby the state sector went co-educational with
little opposition or, indeed, thought. Parents who now
want to exercise their 'right' to choose single-sex education
have to pay for it, if they can. Many grammar schools were
single-sex and their reputations as 'excellent' were often
symbolized by that fact, along with the wearing of
uniforms and use of homework. During times when open
support for grammar schools may not be politically feasible
or admissible a switch of concern to the right to choose
single-sex schooling may achieve the same end. Denominational schools offer a similar opportunity to preserve
class interests one step removed, for they are often also
single-sex and on both counts selective in varying degrees.
In many areas they are the only single-sex schools left.
Issues such as these are always highly localized and bound
up with a number of other considerations such as the dis-
pute over a mixed comprehensive which was closed in the
Edgehill district of Liverpool, apparently on the grounds of
falling rolls and unpopularity with parents despite claims

by the LEA that it was a racially mixed and successful school, in order that an all girls school could be opened on the same site.[17] The falling rolls argument is one used most often against single-sex schools, thus it is unlikely on grounds of sexual equality alone that such a school would have been contemplated.

When choice is promoted as a key issue in education or an essential principle to be defended it is exercised in a way that leads to class, or class interests, taking precedence over gender. An illustration of this, and of Lockwood's social level of integration, is provided by a report from a parent who had attended a meeting called to discuss the London Borough of Barnet's plan to merge two girls schools. Supposedly all the parents had come because they wanted single-sex schooling for their daughters yet— when faced with the choice of amalgamation with a girls school of lower social status or with a boys school of equal social status—the meeting swiftly swung to wanting amalgamation with the boys school.[18]

At a practical and political level, the subordination of gender to class has a number of implications. As Green has argued in a general treatise on the persistence of inequality, the barriers of caste (in which he includes gender) and class require different kinds of attack.[19] Far from class being the most appropriate ground on which to recommend reverse discrimination he argues that the only way to abolish the effects of class differentials is to abolish the differentials themselves. In contrast, caste differentials can be abolished through, and only through, increased group mobility which in turn requires a moral revolution. His argument turns on a number of critical points that need stating. First, that reverse discrimination, quotas or affirmative action is effective in promoting group mobility. Second, that the poor are not discriminated against primarily on the grounds of their poverty but secondarily on the grounds that they have failed, as a result of their poverty, to develop capacities that would have ensured their success. The children of the poor, he argues, no longer need models of inspiration and do not suffer from internalized beliefs of inferiority. Whether or not this is wholly true his argument highlights the role of *mobility* which differentiates class and gender inequality in a fundamental way. For class is a continuous variable whilst gender is not and the implication for individuals are different. Education, however it is organized, *may* help you change your class but it cannot help you change gender.

Earlier in his argument Green observes that it is harder for men to hand down whatever gender privileges they may have to their male children when land is not a key to social status and where the most common public ideology is a generalized rule of formal equality.[20] In such a situation the fathers of daughters are caught between choice of ideologies which justify either subordination or equality and, unless that choice is spelt out openly, they tend to choose the former—often, as the example of the Barnet parent reported above showed, out of a primary commitment to maintaining class identity.

Conclusion

I have argued that in principle co-education represented the most serious challenge to a basically inegalitarian education system that has been mounted or suggested in this country. That is, if it had been carried through. In fact it left the distribution of educational opportunities between boys and girls essentially unchanged and possibly worsened them for girls. It is this fact that needs explanation.

I have also argued that the removal of formal barriers increases both the scope of informal discrimination and the interaction between gender and class. This operates primarily at the level of inter-personal relations which are essentially uncontrolled and uncontrollable. Thus the argument for single-sex school schooling as it affects girls is made on the practical grounds that it uses otherwise suspect categories openly and positively rather than covertly and negatively. Whereas co-education in principle offers equality of opportunity but in fact reduces the opportunity of equality, single-sex schools may offer genuine equality of opportunity in the highly unequal society in which we still live.

Reinforcing these arguments are theoretical grounds why efforts at social change should be directed at the level of system integration rather than social integration which to date has dominated the discussion of educational reform, and in particular of sexism and sexual discrimination in education. Archer has complained that the sociology of education is deficient, having failed to develop a sociology of education systems.[21] The result is that it tends to treat educational institutions as completely permeable and cannot provide an adequate politics of education. Instead schools, and other educational institutions, are thought to simply refract or reflect social processes that originate elsewhere and those looking for empirical detail of how this happens are left with little beyond the ethnography of the classroom. The issue of the inter-relation between sexual divisions, co-educational schools and comprehensive re-organization offers an alternative perspective. First it provides us with an example of the conversion of class dynamics into those of sexual division as mediated by the dominant ideology of individualism and, second, it shows the importance of maintaining organizational boundaries. In a general onslaught on individualism in education Hargreaves[22] has claimed that it has all but evacuated from the formal side of education any positive collective experience, which now survives only in a remaindered form as part of a generally oppositional youth culture. We should add to his indictment the case of co-education insofar as it was thought to be progressive; reject the traditional liberal solution of seaching for better classroom practices to solve a problem largely begat by a liberal individualistic approach to sexual inequality in the first place and be unashamed in our support of single-sex schools.

Notes

1 King (1971).
2 See Gray (1981) and Legrand (1982).
3 Bloomfield and Pratt (1980).
4 Douglas, Ross and Simpson (1968); see also Cherry and Douglas (1977).
5 Weinberg (1979) looks at the shift to co-education as a consequence of comprehensivation.
6 DES (1975).
7 DES (1979).
8 This experiment is discussed in Chapter 5; similar experiments are also being tried by the Tameside 'Girls and Science'. Initiative and information on this can be obtained from Gill Rhydderch, Tameside Teachers' Centre, Waterloo Road, Stalybridge, Cheshire, SK15 1JZ.
9 See Harding (1980).
10 Gray (1980).
11 See Heath (1981) and Hakim (1979) on female social mobility and occupational segregation by sex, respectively.
12 This is considered by Hutchinson and McPherson (1976).
13 Gray (1981).
14 Byrne (1975) looks at differential resourcing of boys and girls schools.
15 Lockwood (1964).
16 *Ibid.*
17 See *The Guardian*, 29 December 1980.
18 See *The Times Educational Supplement*, 18 April 1980.
19 Green (1982).
20 *Ibid.*
21 Archer (1982).
22 Hargreaves (1980). The same argument is more fully developed in relation to comprehensive schools in Hargreaves (1982).

CHAPTER 3

How shall we educate our sons?

MADELEINE ARNOT

'My son talks to me of his new interest reading
adventure/espionage/mystery/space fiction/war
stuff which little boys' and big boys' worlds
are made of
and where women have no place
though i don't tell him this yet
instead i watch him entering
faster and faster
this world (he can't wait till he's eighteen)
the man's world
which circumscribes/denigrates/exploits/obscures/omits
me
and i weep inside myself' 1

This paper will focus upon how we should educate our
sons so that in Adrienne Rich's words they 'grow into
themselves, to discover new ways of being men even as we
are discovering new ways of being women'.[2] It is only
recently that the women's movement in Britain has turned
its attention to 'the problem of men', and as Angela
Hamblin has pointed out, although we may now have a
clearer idea about what we don't want our sons to become,
we have as yet few positive alternative images of maleness
to offer.[3]

The recent feminist analysis of co-educational schools
has also made the discussion of boys' education urgent,
since so much of this research has revealed that, often, it is
boys who are the problem for girls in schools. Studies such

as those by Delamont, Spender and Clarricoates have
shown us how teachers tend to concentrate their time and
energy upon boys in their classrooms, extending more
approval *and* more disapproval to boys than to girls.[4] In
research such as that conducted by Walkerdine, Stanworth
and Fuller, we get glimpses of the extent of boys' disruption of the classroom; their noisiness, their sexual harassment of girls and female teachers, their demands for attention and their need of disciplining and their attitudes to the
girls in their class as the silent or the 'faceless' bunch.[5]

The sexism of boys towards their girlfriends and towards
girls in their class at school also directly affects girls' image
of their future lives and shapes their adolescent culture.
Angela McRobbie has criticized youth culture theorists
such as Willis and Hebdige for romanticizing male working-class culture, by refusing to notice the harmful effects
the 'lads'' aggressive sexual styles have upon girls' self
respect.[6] Dale Spender has suggested that boys' verbal and
physical assaults on girls in school militates against girls'
educational advancement, their freedom to acquire confidence in themselves and their abilities.[7] In this context,
the placing together of both sexes in mixed schools has
been questioned. According to Skinningsrud the ideology
of 'proximity will lead to equality' can be shown not just to
have failed in the case of girls, but even to have led to
reduced chances for girls in the educational system.[8]

In this chapter I shall look at the education of boys in our
school system and discuss the ways in which their education can be perceived as a problem not just for girls, but for
the boys themselves. I shall argue that co-education is not
just a female issue, and that what to do about educating
boys cannot be relegated to a side issue in developing a
feminist analysis of the educational system.

Gender and the two cultures

Up until now those concerned with the pattern of girls'

educational achievement have focused upon the patterns of school subject choice as indicative of the limited and limiting range of their education. What is worrying is the fact that girls have tended to choose and study mainly the arts and humanities, particularly when heading for a higher education. On the practical side, girls have selected or been directed towards the domestic crafts rather than technical and engineering subjects. Undoubtedly the absence of women in the world of science and technology, in high-status professions, in skilled jobs, can be seen as a result of their academic choice of non-scientific disciplines. Further, women, it is argued, cannot understand nor actively participate in our modern technological society, without such knowledge.

But what are the implications of boys' education—an

Fig 3.1 GCE 'O' level entries Summer 1980

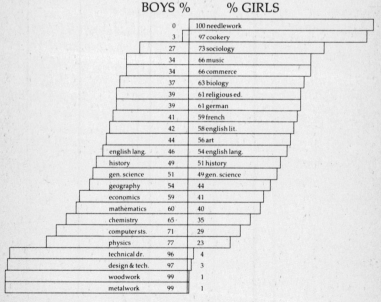

BOYS %   % GIRLS

BOYS %		% GIRLS
	0	100 needlework
	3	97 cookery
	27	73 sociology
	34	66 music
	34	66 commerce
	37	63 biology
	39	61 religious ed.
	39	61 german
	41	59 french
	42	58 english lit.
	44	56 art
english lang.	46	54 english lang.
history	49	51 history
gen. science	51	49 gen. science
geography	54	44
economics	59	41
mathematics	60	40
chemistry	65	35
computer sts.	71	29
physics	77	23
technical dr.	96	4
design & tech.	97	3
woodwork	99	1
metalwork	99	1

Source: Harding, J (1982) 'C.D.T. what's missing?'
Studies in Design Education, Craft and Technology
Vol. 15, No. 1, winter. Department of Education, University of Keele, Stafford-shire. ST5 5BG.

education which is narrowly restricted to the scientific and technical subjects with only a limited involvement in the humanities and social sciences (other than history or English language)? One could argue, from Figure 3.1, that a binary system of education has been established in which science and technology is a male culture and the study of the world of literature, art, languages, religion, music, domestic crafts is a female culture.

It is also well accepted that such patterns of school subject choice at secondary level affect not just 'O' and 'A' level candidates but also CSE students. In 1980 for example in the area of craft studies, 1000 girls compared with 60,000 boys took woodwork and 600 girls compared with 59,000 boys took metalwork.

The process of gender differentiation of the science/arts cultures begins at primary level. The 1975 DES Survey by HMI reported that during 1973 boys in primary schools were far more likely to be offered mechanical toys than anything to do with the home, dressing up, shopping etc. They were less likely to be found in the school choir and orchestra since 'some boys regard music like poetry as "girlish", and because others regard getting into the football team as the more credit-worthy aim, and therefore go to the football rather than go to the choir practice'.[9]

In middle schools boys were likely to be separated from girls for some aspects of physical education and there was a tendency to 'limit experience in the aesthetic aspects of movement to girls, and thus to restrict boys to activities concerned with skill training'.[10] Boys, in secondary schools were more likely to be offered gymnastics rather than dance-based activities; they were offered less opportunities in aesthetic and creative play, in music and to a lesser extent in art, than girls. Even when they could study music however, only one out of ten boys took the subject at secondary level.

The concern for vocational skill-based training for boys for adult life was clearly reflected in the options offered to them in the fourth and fifth years in secondary school. Boys were more likely to be offered specialist pre-vocational and practical courses in, for example, agriculture, building, engineering design and surveying rather than recreational or artistic courses. In contrast girls were offered courses designed to prepare them for the home and for 'female' types of occupations—childcare, child development, mothercare and home-making. They were also likely to be in the majority in the integrated courses in social education and citizenship (e.g. citizenship, humanities, design for living, environmental studies, urban studies and social education). A few options were shared by both sexes— such as accountancy, catering, electronics and fashion design.

The pattern of school subject choice in the school subjects considered 'more academic' revealed that boys linked their choices to future 'male' occupations. In 1975 some 47 per cent of boys took physics and 27 per cent chemistry as fourth and fifth year options, compared with 12 per cent and 17 per cent of girls respectively. A higher percentage of boys chose two science subjects than girls, and a lower percentage of boys took foreign languages. At 'A' level the same year, boys were even more concentrated in the sciences with 41 per cent taking mathematics or physics and only 8 per cent and 3 per cent studying French or German.[11] Only one in five boys took English literature at this level compared with one in two girls. Almost double the proportion of girls studied Art and Music at 'A' level than boys. The DES study was carried out in 1973, two years before the Sex Discrimination Act became law. Similar patterns of sex differences based on more recent evidence can be found in a 1982 report on ILEA schools, and in DES Statistics of Education for 'O' level and CSE subjects.[12]

Differences between boys' and girls' school culture can be related to what feminists have identified as a division between the public and private worlds. As Bourdieu has argued, in European societies, dominated as they are by male values, men have become associated with politics, history and war whilst women are associated with the hearth, the novel and psychology. Other divisions such as those between reason and emotion, science and art, technology and nature, reality and fantasy, objectivity and subjectivity can be seen as derivative and supportive of this public/private division.[13]

The question which concerns us here is how do boys learn to limit their interests to the public sphere, to take such an interest in science and technology and to resist the development of their emotional and artistic selves? Secondly we also need to know what the implications are of such male curricular choices for both boys and girls.

Becoming a man

The processes of learning which are the 'male' subjects are not dissimilar from those experienced by girls learning 'female' educational routes. The former involve the transmission of particular images of masculinity in children's literature, television, popular music, comics and schoolboy magazines, school textbooks etc. Teachers, parents and other children reinforce, through their expectations, the notions of what is 'manly', what is appropriate and inappropriate for boys at different ages. The processes of learning involve also moving from the world of early childhood male heroes to the more realisable dreams of adult male life. This process I have described as one of 'recontextualization' through which the models of masculinity used in the family, home and in mass media are transformed into the more school-based forms of masculinity, such as 'doing science' and learning how to play football.[14]

The pattern of recontextualization occurs also with the help of the often hidden bias of school materials. As Alison Kelly and others have noted, school science textbooks are filled with masculine imagery, through their choice of photographs of males, examples drawn from the male world, styles of learning and assessment which favour male students, and an impersonal approach which tends to suit boys more than girls.[15] If most science students are male, it is hardly surprising since the occupations envisaged for the successful science student are those currently dominated by men.

Within the family also, as Alison Kelly *et al's* recent study has shown, both working-class and middle-class parents were far more concerned that their sons took science and craft subjects rather than the less vocational subjects such as languages, Arts and domestic subjects.[16] Further when it came to giving help with school work the science/arts division was reinforced by the mother helping her son with English and the father helping him with mathematics. In neither social class were boys encouraged to wash and mend clothes, cook, clean the house or wash up. The most they might be asked was to help with the shopping and tidy their own rooms and clean their own shoes. Families, therefore, were likely to develop the need for boys to have full-time 'house' wives to look after them in adult life.

Parental expectations of boys' lives are also reinforced by other aspects of school life such as careers guidance. The EOC, for example, found that school careers literature depicted men and boys too often as 'independent, active, strong and interested in their work', whereas they could be portrayed as sensitive, caring and with their own domestic commitments.[17]

Furthermore the sex-segregation of teaching staff by subject is also likely to reinforce a boy's view that certain subjects are not 'masculine'. In 1977, for example, in secondary schools, male teachers constituted only 1 per cent of the home economics teaching staff, 38 per cent of the French and 44 per cent of English teachers compared with 99 per cent of craft, design and technology course teachers, 88 per cent of physics and 82 per cent of chemistry teachers.[18]

The ideology of masculinity and its implications

Let us now return to the question I raised earlier. What are the likely implications of a pattern of sex-divided school subject choice for boys and girls? The first and most direct implication is that by their limited exposure to the arts, the humanities and social sciences boys are not encouraged to think about human values, wider social issues and their personal lives. They concentrate upon obtaining skills for living in only one sphere of social life, probably leaving school 'ill-equipped for personal independence and for taking shared responsibility in home and family life'.[19] They are poorly prepared for dealing with people and for dealing with their own emotions.

The more general implications of this pattern of male education is that through subject choices, a specific ideology of the family is being perpetuated. This ideology of the family is one in which men are expected to become the breadwinner and to have a dependent wife and dependent children. In order to fulfil this role, it is a major priority for boys to find themselves an occupation and earn a living, first for themselves and later for their families. The notion of 'education for work' has particular meaning therefore for the reproduction of masculinity. Further, the process of reproducing the link between masculinity and paid work is one which affects not just men but also women. It makes the ideological assumption that women will not be major breadwinners and can therefore be paid less than men for similar work,[20] since they are likely to marry and become financial dependents of men. Women's primary role in life is therefore defined as the care and servicing of the family. Such assumptions and ideologies about boys' education match well those state policies which support the man as head of the household and treat women as dependents of men (e.g. family law, social security, taxation).

The result of ideologies about masculinity is that boys are taught to see their major commitment and interest in life as life-long paid work (or as long as the economy needs them). Unemployment strikes hard at men's definition of themselves 'as men'. Paid work after all is defined as the focus of their lives, and the criteria through which men judge other men. Endless striving for success in the occupational world or in the class cultures which surround and are based in that world, means also that a man's sexuality may be defined by his occupational status. In the USA it has been said that masculinity and success with women is defined by the size of the paycheck.[21] In the context of male working-class life in Britain, the importance of work, of a job and a wage are well-known features of working-class masculinity. The research of Paul Willis on working-class 'lads' attests to the importance for such boys of leaving school as soon as possible to earn a wage and prove themselves *as men*.[22] Middle-class boys, on the other hand, may stay in the educational system into their mid-twenties. Nevertheless, there is a close link between men's salary level and their sense of achievement as men.

The ideology of vocationalism for boys has been one rationale for changes within the state school system since the nineteenth century. As Wolpe has shown, the *common code* of government thinking has been that boys' main interests ought to lie in the world of paid work and that a school system could and should be designed to cater for skill differences within that world. The social class differences in educational attainment of boys therefore were and still are seen as more significant than those of girls (all of whom could be assumed to become wives and mothers).[23] The ideals of meritocracy can also be seen as ideals of a male meritocracy, encouraging amongst boys a sense of individualism, competitiveness and materialism. In this context, the labelling of some as academic 'successes' and others as 'failures' by teachers and through examinations has had particular significance for boys *as* boys. It is to this psychological level that I will now turn.

The problem for boys

There is a body of opinion that has worried over the effects of such educational patterning for boys' mental health and emotional stability. This is particularly the case in the USA where the 'masculine mystique' is considered to lead to a variety of social problems. Steinem for example, quotes the National Commission on the Causes and Prevention of Violence who reported that the USA is the 'clear leader among modern, stable democratic nations in its rates of homicide, assault, rape and robbery, and at least among the highest in incidence of group violence and assassination'.[24] Most of these violent crimes are committed by men between 15 and 24 years of age. Proving masculinity, the report explains 'may require frequent rehearsal of toughness, the exploitation of women and quick, aggressive responses'. The masculine ethic is more likely to encourage tough policies of showmanship, of seeking victories especially in American foreign policy: 'Peace at any price is humiliation, but victory at any price—even genocide in Indochina and chaos at home — is quite all right. So goes the Masculine Mystique'.[25]

The link between aggressive political life, militarism, racism and sexism and Western notions of masculinity[26] also has personal implications:

> The first tragedy of this role-playing is personal. Men are made to feel they must earn their manhood by suppressing emotion, perpetuating their superiority over women (and, in racist societies, over non-white men as well), and imposing their will on others whether by violence or by economic means.[27]

The work of the school in imposing these aspects of masculinity is therefore criticized for the unnecessary pressure brought to bear upon boys, academically and vocationally. Lowenstein's report for the National Conference of Parent–Teacher Associations in the United States argued that boys' personal defeats and failures:

> bring about a diminishing of the ego, a self-hatred and sometimes even greater tragedies. Schools are unlikely to see a boy who has neurotically high standards for himself as acting self-destructively.[28]

In 1982 the EOC funded a conference called 'What's in it for boys?', supported by ILEA and the Schools Council. Introducing the report of the conference Leslie Mapp observed that for men to adopt the expected male role and conform to society's notion of masculinity in our society comes at a cost. Men, he argued, pay a price for their privilege. This price includes:

> the suppression of emotion, a predatory sexuality and a level of personal anxiety which demands continual competition to out-perform others.[29]

The opening speaker at the conference, Kate Myers, commented that the traditional masculine values of taking as much pain as possible without giving in, being able to 'hold' alcohol, to show no feelings, to be competitive is hardly likely to fit in with equal participation in parenthood, with valuing women and respecting an equality of the sexes.[30]

According to psychologists such as Horney and Chodorow, boys learn to become men through a process of avoiding, even of coming to dread any association with, the feminine.[31] With an absent father, male children have no male model to copy, only their ever-present mother. The way of achieving masculinity becomes, therefore, a process of devaluing women, of rejecting female objects, activities, emotions, interests, etc. Boys learn to eschew the domestic and to repress the emotional sides of life. Quoting the work of Margaret Mead, Chodorow argues that maleness in our society is never absolutely defined.[32] Unlike femininity, which in a patriarchal society is ascribed, masculinity and manhood has to be achieved, in a permanent process of struggle and confirmation.

In this context it is hardly surprising that it is boys who are the most prone to construct and use gender categories. Not only do they have more at stake in such a system of classification (i.e. male power). Also they have to try to achieve manhood through the dual process of distancing women and femininity from themselves *and* maintaining the hierarchy and social superiority of masculinity by devaluing the female world. When boys come into contact with girls in mixed schools therefore the likelihood is that there will be a considerable polarization between boys and girls, their interests, activities, curriculum choices, friendship groups etc. As Jenny Shaw argues:

> . . . the social structure of mixed schools may drive children to make even more sex-stereotyped subject choices, precisely because of the constant presence of the other sex and the pressure to maintain boundaries, distinctiveness and identity.[33]

The pressure to conform to the masculine ideal and to maintain the gender classification may originally be generated within the home, but soon it is internalized by boys 'who hold both themselves and their peers to account over it'.[34] Male youth cultures become critical elements in 'policing' the boundaries of masculinity. Such youth cultures and male peer groups can also be found in single-sex schools where an imaginary female is constructed to delineate the borders between what is male and what is female. As one teacher in a boys' school described it:

> It seems to me that the boys create an inferior or outside group and level the abuse at them that they would otherwise direct at the girls. The least 'manly' boys become the target and are used as substitute girls in a way.

> In an all boys school a group of 'not-real-boys' gets created. They are called the poofters and the cissies and are constantly likened to girls. The sexual hierarchy gets set up but some boys have to play the part that the girls would take in a mixed school. But of course they are still *all* boys and so the results of the pseudo-girls still stand as the result of boys.[35]

Educational solutions: single-sex or mixed schools?

The solutions to such problems of boys' excessive striving for manhood, their devaluation of women and their personal repression of their emotions more often than not have been laid at the feet of mothers and female teachers who are blamed for their oppressive stance towards boys. Lowenstein, for example, takes the data that feminists have argued shows the bias of teachers against *girls* and argues just the reverse[36] He points out that boys get too much attention from teachers, especially in mixed classrooms since teachers expect boys to be more difficult than girls. Teachers tend to leave girls more alone and pick on the boys. He thinks teachers are reluctant to let boys show warmth or feelings; on the other hand, they punish them for acting in a masculine way. Boys receive more physical punishment than girls, and excessive demands are made of their physical prowess. Teachers speak more harshly to boys. In the late 1960s such a view of male 'emasculation' by female school teachers was particularly current in the USA, where it was linked into the apparent disaffection of male students with the Vietnamese War and with society in general. The feminine environment of the family home and the early years of schooling were seen as the cause as in this example:

> Today's hurt, angry little Johnny, feeling shortchanged by his woman teacher who favours little girls, often learns to hate school, nurses his resentment, and sometimes grows into tomorrow's embittered or maladjusted juvenile delinquent, defiant dope-user, sit-in striker, or draft-card burner who laughs at authority.[37]

Mixed schools were identified as the problem, since here the female teachers could favour their own sex—the notion of the 'good pupil' was the female pupil. Female teachers were portrayed as antagonistic to the opposite sex, said to 'prefer conformity, mental passivity and gentle obedience—at which girls excel—to the aggressive drive and originality of many boys'.[38]

The solution for some was not just to encourage more men to enter teaching at primary level, but also to remove boys from contact with female pupils. Pollack reports an experiment conducted in the late 1960s at Wakefield Forest Elementary School, Virginia, in which separate classes for each sex were set up. Apparently such sex segregation resulted in fewer serious discipline problems. Boys who had been withdrawn became more outgoing and more confident. In health classes both boys and girls were more at ease. The Principal at the time said of the experiment:

> boys are more thoughtful and considerate of each other, wanting to help each other. The lack of distraction from the opposite sex results in better work habits. Boys take part more freely in art and music and do better work in foreign languages when in separate classes. Boys and girls overcome their fear of standing in front of the class to give reports and oral readings.[39]

Despite the beneficial effects upon the pupils, such segregation was based on the reinforcement of the differences between the sexes. Girls were given quieter games, fairy stories, and games and songs which emphasized feminine activities such as sewing and housekeeping. Boys were encouraged, on the other hand, into active physical games, noise and muscle movement based upon 'a transportation theme'.

The segregation of boys and girls in school and between schools is a practice well known in English educational history. Its purpose has been precisely to reproduce a more coherent sense of masculinity and femininity rather than to promote equality of the sexes. However, a continual dilemma of such segregated education has been that male bonding in all boys schools can go too far—leading either to homosexuality or to excessive aggression on the part of the boys. The solution to both these problems has been, for some, the introduction of girls into the major public schools. Girls, in their traditional 'femininity' have been used as a means of 'civilizing' boys—never it would seem has the argument been reversed. But do boys become less stereotyped into masculine traits in mixed schools? Do they widen their education? What the DES Report in 1975 discovered was that boys in mixed schools had less oppor-

tunity to study history, yet more chance to study music and
French and German than boys in single-sex schools. However, in terms of subject choice, boys were more likely to
study history, French and German in boys' only schools.
The tendency overall was, therefore, that boys and girls
were more polarized into the science/arts split in mixed
schools than in single-sex schools. This ties in with the discussion of greater gender differentiation in mixed schools
outlined above.

It must be remembered, however, that boys do well in
either type of school compared with girls. Also, boys of different social classes achieve differentially. Working-class
boys, Douglas *et al.* found at 11 and 15 years of age performed better on reading and mathematics tests in single-
sex grammar schools. Middle-class boys also seem to get an
added advantage in single-sex schools of all school types
(grammar or secondary modern). Overall the sex structure
of secondary modern schools seems to have made little difference to male pupils, in this early study.[40] However, there
did seem to be additional academic advantages in single-
sex grammar school education for boys.

A contrasting advantage of boys' schools lies in a completely different purpose—that of trying to *change* boys'
attitudes to masculinity and femininity and sex roles. In
one school in London (Hackney Downs) teachers have
exploited the single-sex environment of their school to set
up a pilot scheme called 'Skills for Living'.[41] In this project
boys are encouraged to think about such things as food
preparation, shopping and baby care, to anticipate their
future domestic lives. Classes discuss sexism in birthday
cards, children's toys and books. The pupils are also
encouraged to treat each other in a caring way. What the
teachers are attempting is a redefinition of men's role in the
family and a forum for boys to make themselves more
aware of society's and their own assumptions about male
and female roles. Such small-scale experiments point the
way to a large-scale reform programme that could be
developed within single-sex boys' schools.

Yet any reform programme involving the 'emancipation of men' requires more than a restructuring of their school lives, although obviously this is an essential, not a marginal component. The definitions of masculinity which I have talked about are historical products—they are integral to the development of our sort of society. What has emerged with the establishment of a patriarchal and a capitalist society is the division between the public and private worlds (of paid employment and family life), to which I referred earlier. This division has also become firmly associated with the division between male and female in such a way that men are now absent members of their homes, they are seen as the main breadwinner and as the head of a household of economic dependents.[42] Until this structure of family and work life is challenged we cannot expect boys to easily relinquish their notions of manhood, machismo and their devaluation of all that is female. The emancipation of men therefore has to tie in with a variety of other strategies to negate the influence of gender divisions within our lives.

In this context the problem *of* boys and *for* boys of existing definitions of masculinity cannot really be solved by arguing either for single-sex or for mixed schools. The content of what is taught, school ideologies about the relations between the sexes (irrespective of whether they are both present or one sex is absent), the structure of classroom life and the sex of the teacher, all play a part in either contributing or challenging boys' assumptions about sex differences and their own sexual identities. The presence of girls in mixed schools may have different effects on boys' self-image and their attitudes to women than an all boys' school, but it is not clear that either type of school in and of itself will reduce the sexism of boys.

In the short term, programmes for reducing sexism in both types of school are essential. In the long term however, if the overall aim is to remove gender as an organizing variable of educational provision, then one has to challenge the existence of schools based upon a division of the school population according to their sex. This is certainly what the National Union of Teachers decided in 1976 when they argued:

> Boys and girls who are respectively educated in single sex schools are not afforded the same opportunities, and the education available to them will continue to reflect the 'raison d'etre' of the school, i.e. to educate boys and girls according to the needs of boys and girls as if those needs were distinguishable from each other.[43]

The NUT also point out there is a 'sound economic case' to be made in supporting co-educational schools since far more effective use can be made of the resources, the teaching staff, facilities, organizational structures etc. if the two sexes are educated in one school.

A final point needs to be made which is that the definitions of masculinity made available and negotiated by boys are not universal—they may well have their own variant in each social class.[44] The debate around whether to provide mixed or single-sex schools for boys cannot therefore ignore that class specificity. Gender identity can be a form of escape from a position of class subordination; it can be the form through which individuals celebrate personal values in an alienated society. Any reform programme, therefore, has to take account of this placing of gender definitions within a class context and to realize just how fundamental the structure of family life and work life is to both middle-class men and working-class men.

To challenge the results, the repercussions of the division between a male public and a female private world, the division and the hierarchy between the sexes is to take on patriarchy. Masculinity, in all its various forms, is not the same as femininity—it is after all a form of *power* and *privilege*. How we design an educational system to remove that power is an enormous challenge and certainly it will involve a variety of different strategies inside and outside the school. But perhaps—because as Margaret Mead has pointed out, maleness isn't absolutely defined but has to be re-earned every day—the possibility is there that daily intervention by teachers, by parents, by boys themselves and girls will have considerable effect.[45] Male dominance, like class dominance, requires at some point that others 'give consent' to that domination and it is here that we should seek reform. As Hamblin points out:

> Patriarchy depends, for its continuation, on our sons. It needs them to become the next generation of adult male oppressors of women in order to continue to reproduce this system of male supremacy. But what would happen to the patriarchal system if our sons did not carry out this allotted task?[46]

Notes

1 Astra in Friedman and Sarah (1982), p. 249.
2 Rich (1977), quoted in Hamblin (1982).
3 Hamblin (1982).
4 Delamont (1980), Spender (1982a) and Clarricoates (1980).
5 Walkerdine (1981), Stanworth (1983) and Fuller (1980).
6 McRobbie (1980). Among authors included in her critique are Willis (1977) and Hebdige (1979).
7 Spender (1982b).
8 Skinningsrud (1982).
9 DES (1975), p. 3.
10 *Ibid.*, p. 21.
11 The comparable figures for girls supplied by the DES (1975) study were 9 per cent physics, 11 per cent mathematics, 24 per cent French, 9 per cent German.
12 ILEA (1982); *DES statistics on education*, Vol. 2 School leavers, published annually, gives information on GCE and CSE subjects entered and passed by both sexes. Additionally, Vicky Ling—an MPhil student at the Department of Social Sciences, Polytechnic of the South Bank, London, SE1—is carrying out research on girls' option choices in five inner London Schools.
13 Bourdieu (1977) and see also MacDonald (now Arnot) (1980).
14 MacDonald (1980).
15 Kelly (1981).
16 Kelly (1982).
17 EOC (1980).

18 See EOC (1982a), p. 10.
19 *Ibid.*, p. 3.
20 The Equal Pay Act 1970 makes it illegal to pay one sex less than the other for equal work. But if employers regrade similar work for each sex differently, then no case for equal pay is answerable.
21 Gould (1974).
22 Willis (1977).
23 Wolpe (1976).
24 Steinem (1974), p. 135.
25 *Ibid.*, p. 137.
26 For other analyses of this theme see Hoch (1979).
27 Steinem (1974), p. 135.
28 Lowenstein (1980), p. 113.
29 Mapp (1982), in EOC (1982).
30 Myers (1982), in EOC (1982).
31 Horney (1932) and Chodorow (1971).
32 Chodorow (1971) and Mead (1949).
33 Shaw (1976), p. 137.
34 Chodorow (1971), p. 186 and see also Hartley (1974).
35 Quoted by Spender (1982a), p. 121.
36 Lowenstein (1980). The research to which Lowenstein refers is reviewed by Lobban (1978).
37 Pollack (1968), p. 21.
38 *Ibid.*, p. 21.
39 *Ibid.*, p. 25.
40 Douglas and Ross (1966).
41 Reported in EOC (1982a), and *The Sunday Times* 20 March 1983, p. 13. See also Moore (1981) and National Association of Youth Clubs (1981) for discussion of youth work projects for boys.
42 For more detailed discussion of this point see Tolson (1977).
43 NUT (1976).
44 Such an analysis is further developed elsewhere, see Arnot (1983).
45 Mead (1949).
46 Hamblin (1982).

CHAPTER 4

The realities of mixed schooling

STANTONBURY CAMPUS (BRIDGEWATER HALL) SEXISM IN EDUCATION GROUP

The Sexism in Education Group at Stantonbury has been in existence for three years now. Stantonbury Campus is an education and leisure complex comprising two large comprehensive schools, Bridgewater Hall and Brindley Hall, into which extensive community facilities are integrated. In 1979 several new staff who had been involved in the women's movement in other places joined the school and were hoping to find some type of women's group. There was also a member of staff who had spent a year determinedly but isolatedly talking about sexism who was pleased to be joined by colleagues with like minds.

Our initial move was to put up posters and to leaflet the pigeon holes of women staff advertising a meeting. We had some pre-conceived idea of what sort of group we wanted, but were prepared to see what the women staff felt to be most appropriate. The fact that this initial meeting was women-only seemed to be the biggest bone of contention at the time. The response to the meeting was huge; we were the butt of many jokes and snide comments but, more positively, fifteen women came to the meeting.

The outcome was that there should be two groups; one was to be a women-only consciousness-raising group, meeting outside of school, the second was to be a mixed group concerned solely with education and meeting within the school.

At the first meeting of the school group, we sat down to try and write a list of the areas with which we were most concerned. These were:

1 Staffing: (a) teaching; (b) ancillary.
2 Classroom interaction.
3 Sexual harassment.
4 Division of girls/boys in both administration and curriculum.
5 Extra curricular activities.

The group was fairly loosely organized. We agreed that we shouldn't have a chairperson or the standard 'meeting' type of organization. This was a mixed blessing. The positive side was the sense of collective responsibility felt by the members of the group; the negative side of this was that we were not always terribly well organized and had no real records of our meetings.

During the first year our activities were fairly wide-ranging. We had people in to talk, attended the Open University Women's Forum, the ILEA 'Sexism in Education' meetings in Clapham, the 'Girls into Science and Technology' project in Manchester, and visited the Werkplatz School in Holland.

Within the school we:
1   Examined the curriculum materials produced by the different departments. We were able to identify examples of bad practice but not always able to convince people of our opinions. This meant that the curriculum revisions that did take place were largely within the faculties where members of the group worked.

2   Considered the way option choices worked. Not surprisingly, an analysis of choices revealed a very stereotypical pattern. Another significant point was that any group that had a wholly CSE tag was predominantly girls and 'O' level groups were predominantly boys, with girls opting

for biology within the sciences, and cookery and house-craft within the technology faculty.

3   Analysed the staffing structure, in terms of the number of women teachers as a proportion of the whole staff, and the distribution of scale points and responsibilities across the sexes.

4   Discussed teaching methods.

Generally, during the first year we felt that we had a lot of impact in that we met with continuing hostility from a number of staff! This varied from very personal attacks on individuals to general lampooning within the school. However, we began to feel that although we were putting a good deal of work into the group we did not actually have any power because we were not a recognized working party. We decided, therefore, that we should present our opinions, findings and proposals at a general staff meeting, where we would ask for the incorporation of a non-sexist statement into the school policy. This meeting was held in the Christmas term of 1982, two-and-a-half years after the original formation of the group. The staff meeting con-sisted of a presentation of our findings to the whole staff and then small group discussions with report back after-wards. The outcome was that our policy statement was accepted and an official working party formed with rep-resentatives from each faculty.

We hoped that having official status would mean that our findings would have to be taken seriously and acted upon. However, inevitably it also heralded in a totally dif-ferent type of structure. A chairperson was appointed from within the group by the headteacher and we were forced into adopting a more formal structure with minute-taking.

Our brief for this phase, established at the full staff meet-ing, was as follows:

Ways forward:

1   Full and detailed review of the curriculum.
2   Establishing sexism as a criteria for curriculum review in all areas.

3   Ensuring that issues of sexism were raised regularly at faculty meetings.
4   Monitoring of the progress of students by sex.
5   Review of all externally published literature used in school.
6   Review of materials used, work done and advice given in careers and tutorial.

We were also asked to write a detailed report for all staff, with definite proposals for action.

Since the initial staff meeting and the setting up of the working party this brief has been broadly followed, though in all six areas there is a good deal of work still to be done. In the intervening period there have been a number of important structural changes in the way the school and the curriculum are organized. In the area of staffing, whilst the situation is still far from equitable across the sexes, the imbalance has been partially redressed over the last year through the giving of a number of key positions and promotions to women. Within the Faculty of Science and Design both areas have moved away from the traditional offering of a range of subjects at CSE and 'O' level, from which students chose or into which they were directed, and instead have provided mixed ability courses in both integrated science and design. This is obviously a big step towards the breaking down of sex-stereotypical option patterns generally found in these areas of school curricula. In the first two years of the school, rigid subject boundaries have been even further weakened through the creation of tutorial curriculum teams which include teachers from the whole range of subjects that the school offers. Generally, there is a move occurring in the school towards greater integration both of subjects in the curriculum and the tutorial–curricular functions. It is felt by the group that the breaking down of traditional stereotypical subjects and structures in this way may have important implications for the creation of a non-sexist education and the experience of girls in a mixed school setting.

There have been two main levels at which the 'non-sexist' group has worked within the school. On the one hand at a public level, as a pressure group, publicizing, promoting and fighting for schoolwide changes in policy and practice, and the other , at a more private level, as a set of individuals working with students and colleagues in their own particular areas of the school. The rest of this chapter is concerned with the subjective experiences of some of the members of the Non-Sexist Education Working Party. The various members of the group have particular interest in different areas of the curriculum and what follows are some of their experiences, findings and proposals.

English

English is a subject where girls have always succeeded, and Bridgewater Hall is no exception, for the girls tend to work harder, write more, show a greater level of commitment and frequently obtain outstanding examination results.

The pattern is one which is very familiar to English Departments, but it gives no reason to be complacent because the corollary is also a familiar one where English becomes down-graded and is regarded as an 'easy' subject. This is particularly true when candidates are examined through Mode III syllabuses as is the case with our English examinations. There are a number of complex reasons, of course, why English attracts dismissive references, but the success of girls may well be an important contributing factor.

As well as being alert to any down-grading of English as a subject, it is most important for us to examine the resource materials which may be implicitly sexist. We can face real dilemmas here, for very often those books which are successful in the classroom because of their lively plot, their humour, their interesting characters, etc. are those very same books which may not be ideologically acceptable because of their sexism. For example, *The Machine Gunners*, an immensely successful and enjoyable book which has some quite subtle points to make about war and what constitutes theft, nonetheless has some horribly stereotyped female characters—' "Is there really?" said Audrey, all eyes and woman for once . . .'—and it is not always entirely clear whether the author, a very sympathetic presence elsewhere in the novel, is entirely aware of the way in which women are being presented. Such disparaging remarks about women and girls, whether the author is aware of them or not, cannot be overlooked if a non-sexist policy is to mean anything at all. On the other hand one is loath to consign books which are otherwise fruitful and enjoyable to the abyss. The only way out is to use the implicit sexism and turn it on its head by discussing it, pointing it out, attacking it, asking about it. It cannot be ignored, since to ignore it is to condone it. In a school where so may people are committed to a non-sexist policy, it is gratifying to note how often students themselves will latch on to the inherent sexism of a text.

There is nothing wrong in using a text in this 'double' way—for the strength and momentum of its story, and also to promote an awareness of its ideology. English Studies have always encouraged a critical appraisal of the mass media (students are encouraged to analyse the 'messages' implicit in advertisements, magazines and newspapers) and so it would seem to be a natural continuation to examine the values that are being purveyed in any literary work. Students are sophisticated beings who can enjoy and be gripped by a story, while appreciating and deploring the messages which may be implicit in that story. That is not to say that 'anything goes' either, for literary merit is always desirable and we are not too keen on the idea of war comics and soft porn in any classroom, no matter how 'critical' the atmosphere may be.

Most important to English teaching is discussion among members of the teaching team to promote in one another an awareness of sexism in teaching materials and teaching methods and also discussion between teachers and students so that sexism is noted wherever it occurs. The materials used (which we usually write ourselves) also need to be carefully monitored.

It is interesting to look at the differences that can be found in written work completed by boys and girls. Any English Literature Examiner can testify to the way in which boys often produce short, elliptical answers in exam conditions, whereas girls write longer, more detailed answers. Similar differences appear in Mode III folders—the sheer *weight* of some girls' folders is phenomenal. This is obviously a generalization, but the trend does seem to exist as does the difference in subjects chosen for creative writing when students are given a free choice. For instance, the romantic essay is alive and well:

> Then we went away to the Bahamas for a sunny holiday, to make a new start. He paid for every little thing on the holiday, the only thing I paid for were a few clothes that I bought to make Terry feel proud of me.

As is the war story:

> The mercenaries just stared at the dead men. They were all cold, mindless bastards. The RSM produced a cigar, bit the end off, still staring at the dead man.

and the sex of these writers is not too difficult to guess.

However, we hope that by individual discussion, careful drafting and redrafting of work, supportive comment and judicious advice, we may be able to shift the stereotypes a little. It is not quite so easy to work out the sex of the following writers:

> Softly giggling, leaning on each other, Caren and Catherine wobbled back towards his cabin. The door swung softly open, gliding on frictionless hinges.

> Mark: Hello Lisa, I am Mark. I'm your blind date (thoughts . . . she's so handsome and muscular. She's so wonderful, such a woman!)
> Lisa: (Thoughts . . . yuck, such a little wimp—I won't use that dating service again) Hello Mark, nice to meet you . . . .

The time was eleven pm. Everything was black except for the fire from the shells and the constant stream of bullets from our machine guns. At midnight the firing stopped and everything went quiet. We just sat there on guard, waiting for something to happen, but it didn't.

The individualized approach of the Mode III examination where students are completing a personal folder is obviously very important if a student is to move away from formula writing and towards genuinely thoughtful and creative personal writing which eschews stereotypes.

Discussion, dialogue, a careful book-buying policy, together with sympathetic Mode III exam syllabuses, are all central, therefore, to the implementation of a non-sexist policy in English.

Mathematics

The findings of the working party established that girls within the school are underachieving in mathematics and that the situation needs to be remedied. The faculty's search for suitable strategies to remedy the situation, after the working party had drawn attention to the problem, was helped by the findings of the Cockcroft Report in 1982,[1] and several staffing changes.

Suggestions for action can be divided into two broad categories. There are those which assume the problem to lie with girls rather than the subject teaching and the resulting effort is designed to push the female students towards mathematics (girls conforming to subject needs). Others look at the needs and experiences of girls and look for ways to make mathematics more relevant and interesting or understandable for girls (subject moving towards students' needs). The consensus of opinion in the faculty falls firmly behind the second view, although this involves countering the assumptions of boys (and colleagues, parents and industry) about the subject and obviously has a number of far-reaching implications in the classroom.

The failure of the subject to capture the imagination of most of the female students within the school becomes apparent with the very low number of girls wishing to study the subject at 'A' level, although these are implications of our failure throughout the school. Our search for a strategy to remedy this situation is subject to a number of constraints, both positive and negative. The mathematics staff is comprised of both female and male teachers sharing responsibilities and teaching at all levels of the school. In addition we have a very good careers advice system which makes children aware from the third year of the utilitarian advantages of success in mathematics, and refuses to direct girls and boys along sex-stereotyped career paths.

It is usually boys who are visibly and vocally inattentive in any subject. Hence much maths teaching is directed towards the interests that boys exhibit, leaving areas untouched that might provoke a positive response from girls. The same vocal attitude of the male class members demands, and generally inevitably gets, more teacher attention. We have been unable to find a suitable solution to this problem.

There are convincing arguments to suggest that girls achieve greater success in mathematics when taught in single-sex groups (see Chapter 5). There are, however, implications of single-sex setting that do not fit into the Stantonbury philosophy of mixed ability teaching, and certainly the move to full setting on the basis of gender has never been suggested within the school.

However, it is our belief that the faculty needs to take the initiative in finding a curriculum balance within the subject that will serve the requirements of all students. A move towards a two-year experiment teaching certain classes in single-sex groups received considerable support amongst the members of the faculty although it is doubtful whether the reasons for this have been fully appreciated elsewhere in the school. Gut reaction tells most people 'No'.

Our aim would be to pay respect to and take advantage of all the wide range of skills and experiences of our students, not only for girls to feel more comfortable with the mathematics content of the school day, but also to enable boys and girls to develop skills in areas not normally seen as being their domain. To do this we feel we need to establish a dialogue with the girls, to find out how they would like to see their mathematics presented and to develop a suitable teaching strategy.

An example of the effectiveness of bringing together a group of girls to explore maths comes from a very successful event we held in Easter 1983. 'Be a Sumbody' was a one day maths 'event' which aimed to increase girls' involvement in maths by presenting mathematics topics in a new, exciting, practical and relevant way. We had intended to involve teaching staff from every school in Milton Keynes, but although the 130 students came from seven of the eight secondary schools in the city, all but four of the staff involved came from Bridgewater Hall. The event followed similar events staged by the Open University in 1982. Each of the participants was asked to choose two workshops from a prospectus of twelve. These workshops covered a range of interdisciplinary areas. There was a drama workshop, asking students to make quantitative decisions about the siting of a dam in central Africa; a music option, meshing micro-computers with recorders and percussion; groups working on the mathematical relationship of patterns in nature, mathematical puzzles, quantity surveying and a lot more. To conclude the day we arranged a careers convention with women representatives of mathematically based jobs within Milton Keynes. This proved to be a successful practical attempt to involve girls in mathematics, and also served to focus the attention of members of this school and the other schools in Milton Keynes on to the problem of girls' under-achievement in maths.

Science education—did she drop out or was she pushed?[2]

For some time there had been increasing dissatisfaction

within the Science Faculty over the 'option system', whereby the three separate sciences (physics, biology and chemistry) were offered to 'O' level and CSE. In addition we ran a CSE course called 'science' for the least able. All students had to do at least one science subject. If they chose physics or biology or chemistry as this subject, then they could also choose to do one or both of the remaining two.

Several months of discussion by the Campus faculty, at that time composed of three women and ten men, resulted in the opinion that we needed to change to an integrated science course whereby all students did aspects of all three sciences to 16+. At this time the Campus as a whole was attempting to implement a common core curriculum for all students up to fifth year, and the Science Faculty move should be seen within this context.

Initially there was not universal support for this move within the Science Faculty, but after several more discussions we all agreed to develop such a course. The course is a Mode III one, at both 'O' level and CSE (i.e. the syllabus the examinations are set, assessed and marked by the school, with the Examinations Boards overseeing and moderating these procedures).

One of our prime reasons for introducing integrated science into the curriculum was to remove the traditional schism of gender distribution within biology, physics and chemistry. We had always discouraged the view that 'biology is for girls and physics and chemistry for boys'. Nonetheless, in the 'free option' system our biology classes were still dominated by girls and the physics and chemistry classes, by boys. Presumably this was for the reasons that are often cited: peer group pressure; parental pressure; the girls' and boys' self images and their images of the subjects, etc. We hoped, in our case, that it was not due to teacher expectations!

In the Spring of 1981, we set about writing the syllabus. The faculty, as all Science Faculties, consisted of subject specialists and so we ensured that the biology, physics and chemistry input was more than adequate to provide a thorough basis for 'A' levels in these three sciences. There were then six biologists (three female and three male) and seven physicists and chemists (all male). This may, in part, have contributed to the gender divide in students' option choices previously. However, with no empirical studies on this, it is not possible to comment further.

In the first year of the new course (1981–2) we started teaching it to the fourth year in subject-specialist groups. However, over that year we became increasingly committed to the idea that if we were teaching a course of integrated science, then we should see ourselves as 'integrated scientists'. From September 1982, our new fourth year groups have been taught all topics, whether physical or environmental, by one teacher.

The change to becoming 'integrated scientists' has involved considerable in-service training in areas where some of us were previously inexperienced. We have sought to increase our skills, expertise and competence in these areas and so gain the confidence necessary to teach them.

We have certainly removed the traditional gender distribution of students within the three sciences over the last two years. However, this alone is not enough and must be consolidated by combining it with other strategies. Teaching all students all science disciplines is very much undermined if the teaching materials to which they are exposed are sexist in content, presentation and style. Our 'bought in' resources (textbooks, work books, etc) are often sexist, as most science textbooks tend to be (i.e. in most diagrams of people 'doing' things, that person is nearly always a male—the male chemist and the explosive mixture, the male physicist and the telescope, and so on, the examples are legion; the women in such diagrams are usually portrayed in a supportive or ancillary role, even sometimes as purely decorative.) There is not time here to discuss this in more detail, and it is an issue which has been written of at length elsewhere,[3] but nonetheless it is important that the point should be made.

In the Science Faculty, we write a great deal of our own

resources—booklets, worksheets, and so on. Here we are making real attempts to ensure that these materials are non-sexist. This has involved much 'consciousness raising' on behalf of faculty members, and inevitably we still fail at times. Some have argued that students do not notice whether materials are sexist or not; unfortunately this may be true, but they certainly do notice if materials are deliberately non-sexist! Our home-produced resources which begin: 'A scientist was conducting an investigation. She . . ', rarely pass unremarked upon by at least some students in the class.

What effect this 'noticing' has is of course difficult to ascertain; but at the very least it challenges many students' presuppositions about 'male' and 'female' tasks, and the traditional role models with which they are so frequently presented whether in school, by their parents, or through the media.

Finally, the teaching staff must be aware of sexism within their teaching. If we continue to perpetuate stereotypes within science, then as much as our integrated science course may meet its other aims, it will fall short over this. There is little point teaching girls and boys the same subjects if they are treated differently within the subject lessons. One of our then fifth form students carried out a survey amongst forty fifth form students a year ago as part of a Community Education study. We are grateful to her for allowing us to quote her conclusion:

> Although Stantonbury does not encourage discrimination, 74 per cent of girls and 64 per cent of boys said they were treated differently. Girls are allowed to do the same subjects as boys, but they are treated quite differently in the classroom.

Our current concerns rest, amongst other things, with how our new course will affect the gender distribution within future 'A' level sets. Our present fifth year will be the first year to have followed the course through and so it is too early to comment. Will their expectations and image of science have changed in any way as a result of following the course? At present the 'A' level set numbers are as follows:

'A' level Biology: UVI—eight—all female; LVI—sixteen—twelve females, four males.

'A' level Chemistry: UVI—twelve—six females, six males.

'A' level Physics: UVI—eighteen—two females, sixteen males; LVI—Twenty-nine—two females, twenty-seven males.

It will be interesting to see whether the imbalance within these subjects changes over the coming years.

Recreational studies

The Recreational Studies Department has without question made a determined attempt to make the curriculum non-discriminatory and if one looks superficially at the programme one could easily be led to believe that we have been successful. However, if one looks beneath the surface, the traditional approach to physical education, developed from the dominant view that participation in sport is somehow unfeminine, still prevails.

Over the past four years, the curriculum has changed to involve mixed teaching groups for such activities as badminton, swimming, athletics, tennis and gymnastics. The major games of netball, hockey, soccer and rugby remain the domain of the sex they were developed for and are taught in single-sex groups. There are, however, many girls who would like to play soccer and rugby, and indeed many girls do play these games out of school. Some physical educationalists would be horrified to find that we teach any activities in mixed groups; there are many physical education departments throughout the country where female and male staff do not communicate except to argue about the use of facilities, and no doubt the girls department comes off worse.[4] We have therefore made steps in the right direction, although we seem to have lost from our programme, or reduced dramatically, the amount of time spent on activities such as dance and gymnastics; this is in part due to the female/male staffing ratio.

At the time of writing we have two female and five male staff in the faculty, whereas at the time it was proposed that we change to mixed teaching groups we had four women and six men, making it easier to convince some of the staff of its positive aspects. However, as in the majority of physical education departments where there is one overall head holding the major responsibility, it is most often one of the men—in fact, at Stantonbury both the head and deputy heads of the faculty are male. It is an unfortunate outcome of the education cutbacks that the female staff who left were not replaced, leaving this gross imbalance and, as a result, we believe not presenting a very equal role model to the students.

If one was convinced that at least we were making an attempt with the overt curriculum, the consequences of the 'hidden curriculum' are devastating. Expectations of boys and girls vary dramatically and unfortunately this is being constantly reinforced by awards given by national sporting bodies, where better things are always expected of the boys. This difference in expectations is brought home well by comments such as these:

Boys carry the equipment out.

Let's have a few strong boys to put the trampoline away.

[On cross country] Girls do the short course, it's only a mile or so, you can manage that.

Girls can't do rugby, they might hurt themselves. [How many boys are seriously injured playing rugby each season?]

Too often the expectations are too high for many of the non-athletic boys and this leads to comments such as:

Come on, you're like a big girl.

. . . even the girls can do better than that.

Conclusion

In looking at girls' performances and current developments in some subject areas within the curriculum, we have not tried to give a total picture of girls' experience in a mixed-school setting. Our aim has been to highlight key areas across the curriculum where energy and work for change must be directed.

It is clear that the sexism which is inherent in education must be combatted first and foremost by instilling a greater awareness in the staff of the frequently sexist nature of their interactions with colleagues and students. We must examine our treatment of individuals, our demands upon them and our expectations of them which must counter wholeheartedly the traditional expectations decided in our society by gender. Our own attitudes within the classroom give a clear message to students about the differing values we place on girls and boys. Boys, in nearly all situations, occupy more space, make more noise, and regularly demand more from the teacher. It is only the teacher's conscious efforts that will begin to reduce this differential.

To reinforce our classroom behaviour, we must monitor all our materials and resources for stereotypical gender images and introduce male and female characters into roles normally outside their domains. Non-sexist resources should be highlighted and discussion of them encouraged in the same way that we would hope to encourage a critical appraisal of underlying sexism in an otherwise commendable text.

We must continue to be aware of the importance of female role models within the school and encourage women to both take up posts of responsibility and where possible to move into non-traditionally female areas.

In reviewing the curriculum structure as a whole it is important to be mindful of and try to avoid the appearance of sex-stereotypical 'options'. This may well involve the creation of new subjects through the amalgamation and integration of existing subjects.

As a group we were aware at the outset of the need for change in all of these areas, but our experience of three years has sharpened that awareness and taught us a good deal about the mechanics of change.

Notes

1 Cockcroft Report (1982).
2 Heading borrowed from article of the same title, Curran (1982).
3 For example, see Kelly (1981).
4 The area of girls' physical education and sexism in the school curriculum is currently being researched for a PhD by Sheila Scraton in the School of Education, the Open University, Walton Hall, Milton Keynes, MK7 6AA.

CHAPTER 5

Single-sex setting

STUART SMITH

The debate regarding the relative merits of single-sex and co-educational schools has been both long and passionate. Despite the intensity of the argument, however, fair comparisons between the two types of school are almost impossible to achieve. Differing curricula, catchment areas, staff/pupil ratios and teacher qualifications are just four of the variables which make a fair assessment so difficult. Comparisons of academic performance in maths, for instance, frequently indicate that girls in single-sex schools are more successful than girls in co-educational schools, but such comparisons invariably require caution in any interpretation of results.

As an example, in 1964 the NFER applied a series of maths tests to some 12 000 pupils attending all types of secondary school. The results revealed that girls from single-sex schools had a better maths performance in each of the age groups tested compared with girls from co-educational schools.[1] This enquiry qualified these findings by stating that:

> proportionately more secondary modern schools are co-educational than grammar schools, and comprehensive schools tend to be co-educational. These basic organisational facts may explain the differences observed between segregated schools and co-educational schools.

In a piece of research associated with the National Child

Development Study, Jane Steedman noted that girls from single-sex grammar schools did very much better in maths than girls from mixed grammar schools, but she went on to state that 'perhaps it is the case that some of the oldest and least local grammar schools were the single-sex ones; mixed grammar schools were sometimes "creamed" by single-sex ones in the vicinity'.[2]

Similarly, Wood, in a detailed analysis of London Board 'O' level Syllabus 'C' maths papers in 1973 and 1974 found that girls from single-sex schools did rather better than girls from mixed schools, but he went on to suggest that the single-sex schools probably contained a higher proportion of more able girls.[3]

More recently, the 1980 Survey of the Mathematical Development of 15 year olds by the Assessment of Performance Unit suggested that girls from single-sex schools had made more progress in maths than girls from co-educational schools.[4] The APU stressed, however, that these results must be interpreted with care. In 1980, 75 per cent of remaining grammar schools were single-sex compared with only 30 per cent of remaining secondary modern schools and this suggested that a higher proportion of able pupils attended single-sex schools whilst a higher proportion of lower ability pupils attended mixed schools.

Thus, there appears to be a growing body of evidence which suggests that secondary school girls are likely to do better at maths when segregated from boys, yet each piece of this evidence has to be qualified in some way or other. If we are to make a fair comparison of the relative merits of single-sex and mixed classes, it would seem to make sense to look at both types of class within the same school, for in this way many variables can be eliminated.

One school where some interesting work in this direction has taken place is Stamford High School in Tameside. In the mid 1970s Stamford (which at that time was a secondary modern school) suffered a serious problem of widespread under-achievement among girls. This manifested itself most clearly in external examinations. Many able girls, for instance, avoided physics and chemistry and opted for other subjects. Many girls of average ability preferred non-examination courses to subjects which led to the CSE examination. Consequently, total entries for both GCE and CSE examinations were much lower for girls than boys. Furthermore, the average grades achieved in both exams were much poorer for girls than boys.

Although the girls were under-achieving across a broad range of subject disciplines, nowhere was the problem more serious than in maths. In October each year, first year pupils at Stamford were given a maths selection test prior to placement in ability sets. At this stage, there was a close parity of performance between boys and girls and most sets were equally balanced. By the beginning of the fourth year, however (when external examination sets were established), the performance of the girls had declined to such an extent that there were generally only five or six girls in the top (GCE) set compared with twenty-four or twenty-five boys.

Naturally, the girls in this set tended to feel isolated and insecure. They generally congregated in a group on the periphery of the class and were reluctant to participate in oral work. They feared the mockery of the boys and avoided drawing attention to themselves. They greatly preferred familiar, straightforward, repetitive work requiring care and accuracy to any new challenging concepts and problems. The sex of the teacher seemed to have no effect on this pattern of behaviour. Although the girls were reluctant to ask questions during the lesson, they were mostly prepared to query the teacher after the bell. Inevitably, most of the girls in the top set made little progress. It was rare for more than two girls to pass 'O' Level maths whereas Stamford has only once had fewer than twenty boys achieving this target since the introduction of GCE exams.

Naturally, many maths teachers were concerned about this problem, and a meeting of the maths department was held in the spring of 1978 to examine various ideas for improving the performance of the girls. At this meeting, the point that girls in single-sex schools appeared to be more successful at maths was raised and the possibility of establishing single-sex sets was discussed for the first time. Most members of the department believed that single-sex setting would have little or no effect on performance. Nevertheless, it was felt that there was nothing to lose in looking at the effects of single-sex setting and the decision was taken to establish one all girl first year maths set in October 1978. This set would be kept together for two years and its performance would be compared to that of a mixed set of similar ability. Fortunately, the school time-table allowed for the two sets involved in the experiment to be taught maths at different times. Thus, for a period of two years, the two sets were taught similar lessons by the same teachers (one in the first year, the other in the second year). It is important to realize that neither of the teachers involved (both men) believed that single-sex setting would improve the performance of the girls; indeed both then and now, these teachers have expressed personal preferences for teaching mixed sets.

The special setting arrangements were not discussed beforehand with either the pupils involved or their parents, for the school was determined that the courses should proceed quite normally and should not be a focus of attention. In the event, the girls in the all-girls set accepted the setting arrangement quite naturally as they were all new to the school. Similarly, the school received no comments from their parents.

No attempt was made to compare the performance of the two sets in the first year. In the second year, however, the two sets sat three identical maths tests and the results were compared. The first two tests (held in November and February) were wide ranging with emphasis being placed on recently covered topics. The third test (held in June) was the end of year examination and included all topics covered during the year. Average marks (all percentages) are shown in Table 5.1.

Table 5.1 Single-sex and mixed maths sets year 1 and 2 1978–80.

	October 1978 *(initial* *selection test)*	*November* *1979*	*February* *1980*	*June* *1980*
All girls set	58.9	55.1	54.7	51.6
Girls in equivalent mixed set	58.0	50.0	43.9	38.1
Boys in equivalent mixed set	59.0	59.0	56.4	49.3

The October 1978 marks indicate that there was little to choose between the girls in either set at that time.

All three tests held in the second year indicated clearly that most of the girls in the mixed set had fallen well behind the boys in the same set; in other words, these girls were conforming to the typical pattern for the school. The girls in the single-sex set, however, consistently achieved a far better average score than the girls in the mixed set. In the first two second-year tests their average scores were slightly below those of the boys in the mixed set, and they were slightly better than the boys in the end of year exam.

A detailed examination of individual marks revealed that whereas many girls in the mixed set were clearly falling behind, most of the girls in the single-sex set were making satisfactory progress. For instance, in the February test, nine of the girls in the mixed set scored below 40 per cent and only four of the thirty-one girls in the single-sex set failed to achieve this score.[5]

It will be apparent that an all-boys set was also established in October 1980 to balance the all girls set. This boys' set was never the focus of attention, for the school had a strong tradition of academic success by boys in maths and the general feeling was that the boys would do well whether there were girls in the set or not. Nor was it possible to give the teacher of the boys' set in the second year an equivalent mixed set for comparative purposes. Nevertheless, the all boys set achieved persistently high average marks on all three second-year tests justifying the confidence of the maths teachers that their performance would not suffer.

What happened to the girls from the all-girls set at the end of the second year? Unfortunately, it was not possible to allow this set to continue intact into the third year, as this would have caused a major timetable disruption. Consequently, the re-setting of maths in the third year led to the girls being dispersed between various mixed sets. The girls are now (April 1983) reaching the end of their five years at Stamford. They have remained in mixed sets for maths, and will be shortly sitting their CSE and GCE exams.

In the recent 'mock' examinations this group of girls performed quite creditably and it is estimated that eight of them should achieve a grade 'C' GCE pass or better in maths. Most of the remainder should achieve a grade 2 or 3 CSE pass. However, these estimates are only slightly better than the estimates for an equal number of girls of similar ability in the same year at Stamford, and it would appear that the two-year experiment has had little long-term effect on the girls from the single-sex set. Nevertheless, it was quite apparent from various discussions which were held with these girls at the end of the experiment that they had all regarded being taught maths in a single-sex set as an enjoyable experience and that they unanimously disliked being placed with boys for maths in the third year.

Many of the girls were recently asked to write down how the maths setting arrangements had affected them. Here are some of Gillian's thoughts:

> When I was in the all girls set, the atmosphere in the classroom was a lot friendlier than it is in the mixed maths set. The girls were not afraid of going up to the front of the class when they didn't understand. Indeed, we would put up our

hands and ask for help in front of all the class. With the boys there, it is difficult to admit you need help. I am not a shy person, but in maths I need a lot of assistance—but I hate to ask for help. I feel my needs are trivial—I would not be afraid of admitting I didn't understand something in an all girls set—girls are more sympathetic—the boys laugh and make you feel stupid, so making you afraid to ask again if you don't understand. I am normally very confident, but the boys unnerve me in maths.

—I went into a mixed set in the Third Year and hated it. I became a lot quieter and whispered to my friend when I didn't understand. The boys seemed to understand so well—I withdrew from answering—my marks fell.

Boys sit in groups together—they shout the teacher over—they keep the teacher with them for ages—my friend and I get fed up of waiting for help and we try to carry on with the next problem.

In the Fifth Year—I feel as if I have been ignored in maths—the boys in our set have taken all the teacher's time. I don't know if the girls in our set are not as intelligent as the boys—I have given up trying to understand on many occasions this year.

I think most teachers would say this is stupid, that there is no excuse for not asking for help—it would be better —to try to work the problem out together as a group, which girls seem to do in maths. Boys don't like giving time up in maths to listen to extra explanations—girls are more patient.

I felt secure and more confident in the all girls maths set.

One might imagine from Gillian's thoughts that since entering the third year she has been taught by maths teachers who are either weak or unsympathetic to girls. This is certainly not the case. Gillian's comments are in fact typical of those made by most of the original members of the all girls set. It is quite apparent after reading of the experiences of all these girls that boys are inclined to monopolize most maths lessons and that this presents a problem to all the maths teachers at Stamford. It needs to be made quite clear at this stage that all members of the maths department at Stamford are acutely aware of the problems that girls face in maths. The attitude of the maths teachers,

and the ways they have tried to help the girls will be outlined later.

Before leaving Gillian and her colleagues from the
single-sex set, one final question needs to be discussed.
The girls were all asked, since they had found single-sex
setting so beneficial, would they not prefer single-sex
schools? The great majority of the set responded by saying
that girls should not be isolated from boys and that mixed
schools provided a better preparation for adult life. In
English, and many other subjects, most of the girls were
not intimidated by the boys because they had more confidence in their own ability. Maths, however, was regarded
as special, particularly because each individual pupil
requires the undivided attention of the teacher from time
to time. If this attention is not forthcoming, then further
progress is stifled. The girls believed that the acquisition of
mathematical skills, which they recognized as being vital
in adult life, was more easily obtained in single-sex sets.

Now it would be foolish to make too much of this one
experiment in single-sex setting. The number of girls
involved was quite small and therefore the significance of
the results is open to question. Nevertheless, the initial
results were interesting enough to persuade the school to
give more attention to setting arrangements. Consequently, in October 1980, with the exception of a small
number of remedial children, all the first year pupils were
placed in single-sex sets for maths.

At the same time, all the girls in this intake were placed
in girl-dominated sets for science (that is, they were placed
in sets of approximately thirteen girls to six boys). The creation of these sets was a response to the observations of
several science teachers that in balanced mixed classes the
boys monopolized the teacher's time, and that particularly
in the first and second year the girls lacked confidence in
practical work. These observations were closely supported
by some of the findings of an HMI enquiry published in the
same year[6] and this encouraged the Science Department at
Stamford to persevere with these controversial setting

arrangements.

At the time of writing (April 1983) this intake of 1980 is over half way through its third year at Stamford. The pupils are still in single-sex sets for maths, and it is planned for these sets to continue through to the end of the fifth year. The girl-dominated science sets were maintained till the end of the second year, but the third year science sets became single sex. Unfortunately, these single-sex science sets cannot be maintained in the fourth and fifth years because of the options systems and other timetable considerations.

The long-term impact of these special setting arrangements in maths and science on both boys and girls will be interesting. Over the next three years, a detailed research programme, which will involve both attitude and attainment testing, as well as a careful analysis of external examination results, is planned. The main thrust of this research will be a comparison of the intake of 1979 (which will have been taught maths and science for five years in orthodox mixed sets) with the intake of 1980.

No serious comparison of boy/girl performance in maths by the intake of 1980 has yet been attempted, but a superficial examination of the results at the end of the second year revealed that in tests of basic mathematical skills, there was a close parity of performance between boys and girls right across the ability range. There was certainly none of the fall-off in girl performance which was characteristic of intakes that had been taught in mixed sets for two years. On the other hand, with more difficult tests involving problem solving skills given to the top sets only late in the second year, the boys did rather better than the girls. This does cause some concern, particularly as this pattern was not found with similar tests held at the end of the first year.

The school has taken care to explain the special setting arrangements fully to parents of the 1980 intake at appropriate induction and consultation evenings, and these arrangements have certainly been well received. Such individual comments which have been made by parents suggest that they appreciate that Stamford is trying to find ways of improving the academic performance of boys and girls. The school governors also approve of this programme.

Within the school, every effort has been made by teachers to treat pupils in the special sets quite naturally, but occasional discussions have been unavoidable. Too many conclusions should not be drawn from these casual discussions, but the one incontrovertible fact to emerge is that single-sex setting is highly popular with the great majority of boys and girls alike.

What has been the attitude of the maths and science teachers at Stamford to the special setting arrangements? To begin with, all of the teachers involved are experienced enough to realize that special setting arrangements are no panacea which will automatically produce droves of enthusiastic female mathematicians and scientists! At best they regard these arrangements as a useful device to give the girls greater opportunity to succeed. Indeed, it is difficult to summarize the attitudes of the teachers involved primarily because most comments have centred on the one or two sets each teacher has taken. Inevitably such comments are highly subjective. Special setting arrangements are recognized as being controversial, and it would be true to say that most of the teachers involved do have reservations. Several of them believe instinctively that in a mixed school, balanced mixed sets should be established as the natural unit for pupils whenever possible. Others are concerned that single-sex sets create greater disciplinary problems.

Despite these reservations, there is a widespread understanding that a long-term research programme followed by an analysis of the results is the correct way to make an objective assessment. Should this analysis reveal that girl performance has improved, and boy performance has not deteriorated, there is no doubt that the special setting arrangements will be expanded, for at the heart of this work there is a genuine concern that girls must be given a fair opportunity to succeed.

With the Maths Department in particular, single-sex set-ting is only one part of a general programme which has been followed for a number of years to assist the girls. The maths teachers have shown an admirable determination to give an equal opportunity to the girls who have remained in mixed sets. The syllabus has been combed on several occasions to eliminate signs of male bias. Similar steps have been taken with test and exam papers. In recent years, more women maths teachers have been appointed, and the department now has an equal balance of male and female teachers. Additionally, strategies for involving the girls more actively in lessons have been discussed frequently in department meetings. Are the girls given a fair share of questions? Are they given long enough to answer? Are they given a hint, a clue, a supplementary question if they fail to answer? Is each girl given a fair share of individual attention? Do classroom seating arrangements need con-sideration? By debating such questions, each maths teacher has been forced to consider his or her own class-room technique.

This programme certainly seems to have borne some fruit as Table 5.2 indicates.

Table 5.2 Stamford High School—fifth year maths—sets 1 and 2 1976–83

| Year | Composition | | | GCE Passes (Grades A, B, C or CSE 1) | | |
	G	B	T	G	B	T
1976/77				1	24	25
1977/78				2	13	15
1978/79	13	42	55	9	24	33
1979/80	19	40	59	1	25	26
1980/81	19	38	57	13	28	41
1981/82	23	42	65	9	29	38
1982/83	30	36	66	15	28	43

It is perhaps worth mentioning that all the intakes shown in Table 5.2 were 'secondary modern'. The school accepted its first all-ability intake in 1980.

Table 5.2 shows clearly both the changing girl/boy ratio and the improving exam performance of girls in sets 1 and 2. Furthermore these improvements have not been made at the expense of the boys. Indeed, the irony of the situation is that a major effort by committed maths teachers has been of benefit to the girls, but the performance of the boys is still considerably better, and the boys still dominate most mixed maths lessons.

Can the performance of the girls be improved further in a mixed class situation? One way forward may be by the establishment of appropriate teacher in-service training programmes. There have been many studies to show that teachers are inclined to discriminate (normally quite unconsciously) against certain pupils in their classes. Frequently this discrimination is against those pupils the teacher perceives as being low achievers, and the discrimination takes the form of giving such pupils less praise or encouragement and a smaller proportion of the teacher's time and attention. In mixed classes, of course, the discrimination is often against the girls, even though the teacher is often unaware that this is the case.

Is it possible to develop an in-service training programme designed to provide an equal opportunity for all members of the class? An American programme called TESA (Teacher Expectation and Student Achievement) appears to go well beyond anything yet attempted in Britain. The main goal of TESA is to give each member of the class an equal opportunity to succeed and the programme systematically attempts to modify the classroom performance of each teacher on the course to achieve this goal. Teachers on the TESA courses work in pairs, and they are trained to code and observe each other in the classroom. In a series of workshops, generally held one month apart, the teachers are trained to develop a series of 'behaviours' in class. These 'behaviours' deal with such areas as the dis-

tribution of questions about the class, length of time given
to answer questions, and the use of praise, encouragement
and supplementary questions by the teacher. The practical
use of these behaviours is developed in the classroom between workshops. It is supported by regular observation
and coding and discussions between the teacher partners.[7]

TESA may not be quite the appropriate course to help
with the many forms of under achievement in Britain's
classrooms, but there is no doubt that it has been enorm-
ously popular and successful in the USA. The course began
in a small way in Los Angeles in 1971. It has expanded
steadily and two additional course centres have now
opened in Ohio and Florida. Tens of thousands of American teachers (at all levels of education from kindergarten to
university) have completed the course and it has influ-
enced the education of hundreds of thousands of pupils. A
careful analysis of the classroom scores of TESA trained
teachers suggests that all pupils have performed better, but
that those pupils originally perceived as 'low achievers' by
their teachers have benefited most of all. Many TESA
trained teachers have testified to an improvement in their
classroom work. Classroom relationships are said to
improve markedly.

Now it is very easy for us to be sceptical about the value
of an American training course, but in reality there is no
room for complacency, for all our schools face discrimination in some form or another. It is not the purpose of this
article to discuss the many forms of discrimination in
British education; however, if we consider sex discrimination, there are still far too many mixed schools which have
as yet made no serious attempt to ensure that girls are
given an equal academic opportunity.

At a school like Stamford, where maths teachers have
struggled hard for years to give the girls an equal chance,
most mixed classes are still dominated by the boys. What
must be happening in those schools which have as yet not
acknowledged they have such a problem? How many
maths teachers regard the reticent behaviour of their girls

as quite natural? At the end of the day, single-sex setting in maths is little more than a device to secure an equal opportunity for girls. As such, it is surely better than a bland acceptance that maths is a boys' subject and that it is acceptable for girls to play a secondary role.

There are of course numerous secondary teachers who continually strive to ensure that the girls in their mixed classes are given a fair chance. Indeed, it is probable that most of these teachers believe firmly in the principle of co-education. Such teachers must convince their colleagues that the academic needs of girls require special attention. Unless we can learn how to give girls an equal opportunity, there is little doubt that single-sex schools will grow in public favour and mixed schools will decline.

Notes

1 Pidgeon (1967).
2 Steedman (1980).
3 Wood (1976).
4 Assessment of Performance Unit (1982).
5 Smith (1980).
6 HMI (1980).
7 Additional information about TESA may be obtained from Mr Sam Kerman, Program Director, TESA, Los Angeles County Education Center, 9300 Imperial Highway, Rm 246, Downey, California 90242, USA.

CONCLUSION

Co-education, equal educational opportunity and change

ROSEMARY DEEM

Our present educational system, struggling to emerge from its inequalitarian past, is based not so much on distinctions of natural ability as on class, sex and race ... such a situation is bad for society, for individuals and for levels of educational achievement and excellence.[1]

The discussion of equal educational opportunities in Britain has tended, especially in the period 1945–75, to be confined to class rather than dealing with either gender or race.[2] In the case of gender, this is at least partially explained by Shaw in Chapter 2 when she says that it lacks the 'political pull' of class, although many attempts have been made since the mid-1970s to bring gender inequalities firmly onto the educational and political agenda, not only by feminists, but by a variety of other groups and agencies, including the Equal Opportunities Commission and the Department of Education and Science.[3] However, given that it is widely felt that educational changes have failed to tackle the worst excesses of class inequalities[4] despite the political prominence given to this issue, it is perhaps not surprising that gender inequalities have persisted too. The reasons for the persistence of gender inequalities have been much dissected, and we do not pretend to deal with more than a tiny part of the explanation for that persistence here.

However, co-education, both ideologically and in practice, does seem to have failed to provide pupils of both sexes (as well as pupils of all social classes and ethnic groups) with even the semblance of equal opportunities, despite the pious hopes expressed by the DES in *The School Curriculum*[5] that:

> the equal treatment of men and women embodied in our law needs to be supported in the curriculum. It is essential to ensure that equal curricular opportunity is genuinely available to both boys and girls.

Furthermore, there is also strong evidence that the shift to co-educational schools has reduced the promotion chances of women teachers.[6] Brehony's account of the co-education debate in the early decades of the century in Chapter 1 indicates that Arnot's (1983) comment:

> At no point historically was there an attempt to set up an equal (that is, identical) education for boys and girls,[7]

may not have applied to the private sector of education but suggests why those early co-educational ideologies were doomed to fail in practice. The search for individualistic solutions to power inequalities between women and men, the focus on social rather than academic or cognitive outcomes, and the failure to see that gender divisions have structural roots which cannot be dissolved simply by a few changes to schooling, are all important empirical and practical reasons why co-educational ideas have failed to fulfil their promise. There are similarly a number of answers to the question of whether co-education as an ideology can ever be made to work, or whether the ideas themselves are based on false premises, such as the notion that equality in education means identical provision for all 11 year olds,[8] when we know that social divisions begin to manifest themselves at a very early stage in children's lives and socialization experiences. Shaw in Chapter 2 says that co-education is unlikely to provide girls with sufficient social solidarity to challenge existing power relations between the sexes, whilst Arnot in Chapter 3 claims that co-education can work if we change the ideas of masculinity and femininity which are transmitted in schooling, rather than simply altering the form of that transmission. Elsewhere Spender[9] has claimed that what is more important than single-sex or mixed schools is that women should teach women and assume control and responsibility for women's education, and Whyld[10] has suggested that sexism is more likely to be reduced in schools where there are organized groups of teachers (like the group who wrote Chapter 4, for example), a sympathetic head, and an awareness that eradicating gender differences is a priority (something clearly present in the school which Stuart Smith writes about in Chapter 5).

This book did not set out to make a firm and definite set of policy recommendations on co-education, nor has it done so. The options presented range from Brehony's historically based argument that since the social and economic determinations of gender divisions and male–female power relations lie in many other social institutions besides schools, co-education can never provide gender equality, to Smith's positive and constructive emphasis on the possibilities of limited improvements in girls' academic attainments in a small range of subjects through the use of single-sex setting in mixed schools. Only Shaw unreservedly advocates single-sex schooling. And indeed it has to be recognized that in a climate of public expenditure cuts, reduced resources and falling rolls, such an option is not especially likely to be taken up in the state sector (except perhaps for grammar schools, where most remaining single-sex schools are, if LEAs move to re-establish these)[11] whilst the recession is causing some private single-sex schools to consider a partial or complete shift to co-education.[12] What other contributors offer, however, is varying ways in which the practices of co-education can be altered and monitored and there have been other and much more detailed attempts made elsewhere to show teachers how this can be done.[13]

Even if the collection were to make clear and firm policy
recommendations, my own experience as a teacher, local
councillor and school governor tell me that educational
changes rarely come about through the wholesale adoption
of someone else's policy solutions (unless these are
imposed by bodies like the MSC), but are more likely to
occur in a pragmatic way through the discussion of a
number of ideas in response to practical problems, just as
Stuart Smith's former school moved towards the adoption
of single-sex setting because girls were under-achieving in
maths. Change may of course be intended; a number of
comprehensive schools developed innovatory approaches
to education because they were concerned about making
comprehensives work and about the motivation of pupils
throughout their stay at secondary school.[14] Whatever the
reasons for change, as Arnot reminds us at the end of Chapter 3, people in some sense consent to the prevailing social
arrangements in any given society and its social institutions. If change is to occur successfully, consent for it must
also be gained, if that change is not to produce confronta-
tion with LEAs, parents, teachers and local communities.[15]
Since it is highly likely that the continuing recession will
ensure, as Moon notes 'that the main burden for supporting innovation and change will fall on the resources of the
school' so far as the state sector is concerned, it is important
that educational ideas are fully discussed by all those
involved with schools, and some measure of consent for
those ideas obtained in a democratic way, even though this
may mean trying to reconcile the sometimes quite different
views and interests of schools, teachers and pupils, as compared to the communities that schools serve.[16]

Furthermore, although our priority in writing this book
has been the necessity for establishing equal opportunities
in schools for both sexes and discussing how co-education
has contributed or could contribute to this, as one point on
the route to a more equitable distribution of power relations between women and men, it must be recognized that

gender is only one powerful social division in our society and that others are class and ethnicity. These two latter divisions may and do cross-cut and intersect with gender divisions in schooling. Hence it may be possible to solve some of our problems concerning the inequitable distribution of power, occupations and wealth (for example, gender discrimination in schools) without tackling all the sources and determinations of that maldistribution, which lie in the roots of the major social divisions, and are also embedded in all our social institutions, not just in educational establishments.[17] Nevertheless, the debate surrounding co-education is an important one for all concerned with inequitable divisions between social groups, and we hope that *Co-education Reconsidered* will allow a debate, which has only been partially re-opened in the late twentieth century, to be continued and developed, and not lost sight of in a harsh, economic and social climate, which may be perceived as ideologically urging that there are more important things to do and think about than gender discrimination and unequal power relations between the sexes.

Notes

1 Rubenstein (1979), p. 7.
2 See *Ibid.*, and Lodge and Blackstone (1982).
3 See DES (1981).
4 *Ibid.*, and Hargreaves (1982) and Shaw (1983).
5 DES (1981), p. 7.
6 Wilce (1983b).
7 Arnot (1983), p. 87.
8 This issue is discussed in a number of places including Rubenstein (1979) and Lodge and Blackstone (1982).
9 Spender (1982a).
10 Whyld (1983).
11 See Berliner (1983).
12 Walford (1983).
13 See for example Whyld's good and very practical 1983 collection of articles on how to reduce sexism across the entire

secondary school curriculum.
14 How six such schools developed and changed is described in
    Moon (1983).
15 *Ibid.*
16 Moon (1983), p. 133.
17 Hargreaves (1982) argues that one of the central problems of
    contemporary industrial societies is the resolution of conflicts
    often arising from power, occupational and wealthy differen-
    tials between various groups and that developing 'solidary
    communities' throughout society, including through radi-
    cally changed comprehensive schools, is one way of trying to
    resolve those conflicts.

BIBLIOGRAPHY

Anon. (1901), Co-education in private schools, *Journal of Education* **XXIII**, 700.

Anon. (1905), Association of Headmistresses Conference, *Journal of Education* **XXVII**, pp. 469–70.

Archer, M. (1982), The sociology of educational systems, in Bottomore, T. B. Nowak, S. and Sokolowska, M. (eds) *Sociology: the state of the art*, Sage.

Arnot, M. (1983), A cloud over co-education: an analysis of the forms of transmission of class and gender relations, in Walker, S. and Barton, L. (eds) *Gender, class and education*, Falmer Press.

Assessment of Performance Unit (1982), *Mathematical development: secondary survey report No. 3*, HMSO.

Badley, J. H. (1900), The possibility of co-education in English preparatory and other secondary schools, in *Board of Education special report on educational subjects*, Vol. 6, pp. 500–75.

Badley, J. H. (1903), Some problems of government in a mixed school, in Woods, A. (ed.), *Co-education*, Longmans pp. 1–14.

Badley, J. H. (1908), Moral teaching in the secondary school: school activities and co-education, in Sadler, M. E. (ed.) *Moral instruction and training in schools*, Vol. I, Longmans pp. 236–43.

Badley, J. H. (1919), A reply, in Woods, A. (ed.) *Advance in co-education*, Sidgwick and Jackson, pp. 8–24.

Badley, J. H. (1923), *Bedales: a pioneer school*, Methuen.

Berliner, W. (1983), Tories ready to back grammar schools, *Guardian*, 5 September 1983, p. 1.

Bloomfield, J. and Pratt, J. (1980), *Guidelines on secondary school reorganisation*, Centre for Institutional Studies, Anglian Regional Management Centre, North East London Polytechnic.

Board of Education (1923), *Report of the Consultative Committee on differentiation of the curriculum for boys and girls respectively in secondary schools*, HMSO.

Board of Education (1926), *Report of the Consultative Committee on the education of the adolescent*, HMSO.

Bourdieu, P. (1977), *Outline of a theory of practice*, Cambridge University Press.

Bremner, C. S. (1901) Bedales, *Journal of Education* **XXIII**, 237–8.

Brock, C. (1930), in Report of the Association of Headmistresses' Conference at Haberdashers' Hall, London, p. 29.

Byrne, E. (1975), *Women and Education*, Tavistock.

Charity Commissioners (1898), The Welsh Intermediate Education Act 1889: its origin and working, in *Education Department Special Reports on Educational Subjects* Vol 2, HMSO, pp. 1–58.

Cherry, N. and Douglas, J. W. B. (1977). Does sex make a difference? *The Times Educational Supplement* 9 December 1977.

Chodorow, N. (1971), Being and doing; a cross-cultural examination of the socialisation of males and females, in Gornick, V. and Noran, B. K. (eds) *Women in sexist society*, Basic Books.

Clarricoates, K. (1980), The importance of being Earnest . . . Emma . . . Tom . . . Jane: the perception and categorisation of gender conformity and gender deviation in primary schools, in Deem, R. (ed.) *Schooling for women's work*, Routledge and Kegan Paul.

Cockcroft Report (1982), *Mathematics counts: report of a committee of enquiry into the teaching of mathematics in schools*, HMSO.

Curran, L. (1982), Science education—did she drop out or was she pushed?, *Spare Rib*.

Delamont, S. (1980), *Sex roles and the school*, Methuen.

DES (1975), Curricular differences for boys and girls, *Education survey No. 21*, HMSO.

DES (1979), *Aspects of secondary education in England: a report by HM Inspectors of schools*, HMSO.

DES (1981), *The school curriculum*, HMSO.

Douglas, J. W. B., Ross, J. M. (1966), Single sex or co-ed? The academic consequences, *Where* 25 May 1966, pp 5–8.

Douglas, J. W. B., Ross, J. N. and Simpson, H. R. (1968), *All our future*, Davies.

EOC ((1980), *A guide to equal treatment of the sexes in career materials*, Manchester.

EOC (1982a), *Equal opportunities for home economics*, Appendix II, Manchester.

EOC (1982b), *Report of conference on Equal Opportunities: what's in it for boys?'*, Manchester.

Ferriere, A. L. (1921), The new schools, in *New era in home and school* **II** (5), 145–50.

Findlay, J. J. (1927), *The foundations of education* Vol 2, University of London Press.

Fletcher, S. (1982), Co-education and the Victorian grammar school, *History of Education* **II** (2), 87–98.

Friedman, S. and Sarah, E. (eds) (1982), *On the Problem of men*, The Women's Press.

Fuller, M. (1980), Black girls in a London comprehensive school, in Deem, R. (ed.) *Schooling for women's work*, Routledge and Kegan Paul.

Gathorne-Hardy, J. (1977), *The public school phenomenon*, Hodder and Stoughton.

Gould, R. E. (1974), Measuring masculinity by the size of a pay-check, in Pleck, J. H. and Sawyer, J. (eds), *Men and masculinity*, Prentice Hall.

Grant, C. (1902), Can American co-education be grafted upon the English public school system?, in Board of Education, *Special reports on Educational subjects*, Vol. II, HMSO.

Grant, C. (1903), Idleness and co-education, in Woods, A. (ed.) *Co-education*, Longmans, pp. 15–32.

Grant, C. (1908), The relative failure of English public schools: the moral benefit of co-education, in Sadler, M. E. (ed.) *Moral Instruction and training in schools*, Vol. I, Longmans Green, pp. 244–50.

Gray, J. (1980), A competitive edge: examination results and the probable limits of secondary school effectiveness, *Education Review* **33**, (I), February.

Gray, J. (1981), From policy to practice, in Taylor, W. and Simon, B. (eds) *Education in the eighties*, Batsford.

Green, P. (1982), *The pursuit of inequality*, Martin Robertson.

Hakim, C. (1979), *Occupational segregation*, Research paper No. 9, Department of Employment.

Hamblin, A. (1982), What can one do with a son? in Friedman, Sarah (1982), *op. cit.*

Harding, J. (1980), Sex differences in performance in science examinations, in Deem, R. (ed.) *Schooling for women's work*, Routledge and Kegan Paul.

Harding, J. (1982), Craft, design, technology: what's missing? *Studies in Design education, craft and technology* **15**, Winter, pp. 4–5.

Hargreaves, D. (1980), A sociological critique of individualism in education, *British Journal of Educational Studies* **XXVIII** (3), June.

Hargreaves, D. (1982), *The challenge for the comprehensive school: culture, curriculum and community*, Routledge and Kegan Paul.

Hartley, R. (1974), Sex-role pressures and the socialisation of the male child, in Pleck, J. H. and Sawyer, J. (eds) *Men and masculinity*, Prentice Hall.

Heath, A. (1981), *Social mobility*, Fontana.

Hebdige, D. (1979), *Subculture: the meaning of style*, Methuen.

Herford, C. (1903), Thirty years in a day co-educational school, in

Woods, A. (ed.) *Co-education*, Longmans.

HMI Series (1980), *Matters for discussion 13: girls and science*, HMSO.

Hoch, P. (1979), *White hero, black beast*, Pluto Press.

Horney, K. (1932), The dread of women, *International Journal of Psychoanalysis*, **13**.

Hughes, R. E. (1902), *The making of citizens*, Walter Scott.

Hutchinson, D. and MacPherson, A. (1976), Competing inequalities—the sex and social class structure of the first year Scottish university student population 1962–72, *Sociology* **10**, (1).

ILEA (1982), Sex differences and achievement, *Research and Statistical Report RS 823/82*, ILEA.

Kelly, A. (ed.) (1981), *The missing half: girls and science*, Manchester University Press.

Kelly, A. *et al.* (1982), Gender roles at home and school, *British Journal of Sociology of Education* **3** (3), 281–96.

King, R. (1971), Unequal access in Education: sex and social class *Social and Economic Administration* **5** (3), July.

Lane H. (1919), Introduction, in Woods, A. (ed.) *Advance in co-education*, Sidgwick and Jackson, pp. ix–xxii.

Legrand, J. (1982), *Strategy of equality*, Allen and Unwin.

Lobban, G. (1978), The influence of the school on sex-role stereotyping, in Chetwynd, J. and Hartnett, O. (eds) *The sex role system*, Routledge and Kegan Paul.

Lockwood, D. (1964), Social integration and system integration, in Zollschan, D. K. and Hirsch, W. (eds) *Explanations of social change*, Routledge and Kegan Paul.

Lodge, P. and Blackstone, T. (1982), *Educational policy and educational inequality*, Martin Robertson.

Lowenstein, L. F. (1980), Normal problems for normal children, National Confederation of Parent-Teacher Associations, quoted in *Education* 1 August 1980, p. 113.

Macdonald, M. (1980), Schooling and the reproduction of class and gender relations, in Barton, L. and Meighan, R. and Walker, S. (eds) *Schooling Ideology and the curriculum*, Falmer Press, 1980.

McRobbie, A. (1980), Settling accounts with subcultures, *Screen Education*, Spring 34, 37–50.

Mansford, C. J. (1903), The personal element in joint schools, in Woods, A. (ed.) *Co-education*, Longmans, pp. 89–103.

Mapp, L. (1982), in EOC (1982b) *op. cit.*

Mead, M. (1949), *Male and female*, Pelican Books.

Moon, R. (1983), (ed.) *Comprehensive schools: challenge and change*, NFER/Nelson.

Moore, R. (1981), Rethinking work with boys, in *Youth in society: challenging stereotypes-changing roles*, National Youth Bureau.

Myers, K. (1982), in EOC (1982b) *op. cit.*

National Association of Youth Clubs (1981) *Rethinking work with boys: a short reading list*, National Association of Youth Clubs, Leicester.

NUT (1976), Equal opportunities for women. Memorandum submitted to NUT Annual Conference.

O'Neill, E. F. (1919), An elementary school point of view, in Woods, A. (ed.) *Advance in Co-education*, Sidgwick and Jackson, pp. 88–99.

Perks, A. (1903), Impressions of a convert to co-education, in Woods, A. (ed.) *Co-education*, Longmans.

Pidgeon, D. A. (1967), *Achievement in mathematics*, NFER.

Platt, S. and Platt, W. (1919), The human aspect, in Woods, A. (ed.) *Advance in Co-education*, Sidgwick and Jackson, pp. 39–51.

Pollack, J. H. (1968), Are teachers fair to boys?, *Today's Health*, April, 21.

Price. M. and Glenday, N. (1975), *Reluctant revolutionaries*, Isaac Pitman.

Public Records Office (1902), *ED109 1863* Bedales School, Petersfield, Inspection, December.

Public Records Office (1911), *ED109 1864* Bedales School Inspection, November.

Public Records Office (1913), *ED109 3782* The Hampstead School of the King Alfred School Society Inspection, June.

Public Records Office (1920), *ED109 2102*, St Christopher's School, Letchworth, Inspection, September.

Public Records Office (1922), *ED109 4232*, King Alfred School, Hendon, Inspection, October.

Public Records Office (1928), *ED109 4233*, King Alfred School, Hendon, Inspection, June.

Rice, C. E. (1903), Practical solutions of co-educational problems in a day-school, in Woods, A. (ed.) *Co-education*, Longmans.

Rich, A. (1977). *Of woman born*, quoted in Hamblin, A. 'What can one do with a son?', in Friedman, S. and Sarah, E. (1982) *op. cit.* p. 239.

Richmond, K. (1919), Boy and girl friendships: a psycho-analyst's view, in Woods, A. (ed.) *Advance in co-education*, Sidgwick and Jackson, pp. 114–24.

Royal Commission on Secondary Education (1895), *Minutes of evidence* Vol IV, HMSO.

Royden, A. M. (1919), Doubts and difficulties, in Woods, A. (ed.) *Advance in Co-education*, Sidgwick and Jackson, pp. 1–7.

Rubenstein, D. (ed.) (1979), *Education and Inequality*, Harper and Row.

Russell, J. (1920), Co-education, in Watson, F. (ed.) *The encyclopaedia and dictionary of education*, Vol I, Isaac Pitman, pp. 357–8.

Sadler, M. E. (1903), Introduction, in Woods, A. (ed.) *Co-education*, Longmans, pp. xi–xiv.

Shaw, B. (1983), *Comprehensive schooling: the impossible dream?*, Basil Blackwell.

Shaw, J. (1976), Finishing school—some implications of sex-segregated education, in Barker, D. L. and Allen, S. (eds) *Sexual divisions in society: process and change*, Tavistock.

Shaw, J. (1980), Education and the individual: schooling for girls or mixed schooling–a mixed blessing?, in Deem, R. (ed.) *Schooling for women's work*, Routledge and Kegan Paul.

Skinningsrud, F. (1982), Education for equality—the similarity in strategies for eliminating class, gender and ethnic differences in education, *Nordish Forening for Pedagogisk Forskining* No. 1–2.

Smith, S. (1980), Should they be kept apart?, *Times Educational Supplement*, 18 July, 1980.

Spender, D. (1982a), *Invisible women: the schooling scandal*, Writers and Readers Co-operative.

Spender, D. (1982b), What girls learn in mixed sex education, *Tidskrift for Nordisk Forening for Pedagogisk Foorsknining*, **1982**, 1–2.

Stanworth, M. (1983), *Gender and schooling*, Hutchinson.

Steedman, J. (1980), *Progress in mathematics*, National Children's Bureau.

Steinem, G. (1974), The myth of masculine mystique, in Pleck, J. H. and Sawyer, J. (eds), *Men and masculinity*, Prentice Hall.

Stevens, A. (1983), Single sex schools are no better, *The Observer* 7 August 1983.

Stewart, W. A. C. (1968), *The educational innovators*, Vol II, Macmillan.

Tolson, A. (1977), *The limits of masculinity*, Tavistock.

Walford, G. (1983), Girls in boys' schools: a prelude to further research, *British Journal of Sociology of Education* **4** (1), 39–54.

Walkerdine, V. (1981), Sex, power and pedagogy, *Screen Education*, Spring 38.

Wedgwood, E. (1919), A parents point of view, in Woods, A. (ed.)

Advance in Co-education, Sidgwick and Jackson, pp 52–62.

Weinberg, A. (1979), Analysis of the persistence of single-sex secondary schools in the English Education system. Unpublished PhD thesis, University of Sussex.

Weinberg, A. (1981),Non decision-making in English education: the case of single-sex secondary schooling. Paper presented to the British Sociological Association Annual Conference, University College of Wales, Aberystwyth.

Wells, S. (1897), The secondary day school attached to the Battersea (London) Polytechnic—an experiment in the co-education of boys and girls, in Education Department *Special Reports on Educational Subjects* Vol I, HMSO, pp. 196–206.

Whyld, J. (1983), *Sexism in the secondary curriculum*, Harper and Row.

Wilce, H. (1983a), Speaking up, but still faint: the performance of the much criticized Equal Opportunities Commission, *Times Educational Supplement*, 29 April 1983, p. 8.

Wilce, H. (1983b), Continuing fall in number of women who become heads, *Times Educational Supplement*, 29 July 1983, p. 1.

Willis, P. (1977), *Learning to labour*, Saxon House.

Wolpe, A. M. (1976), The official ideology of education for girls, in Flude, M. and Ahier, J. (eds) *Educability, schools and ideology*, Croom Helm.

Wood, R. (1976), Sex differences in mathematics attainment at GCE Ordinary Level, *Educational Studies*.

Woods, A. (1903), (ed.) *Co-education*, Longmans.

Woods, A. (1903), the dangers and difficulties of co-education, *Ibid*.

Woods, A. (1904a), Co-education, *Journal of Education* **XXVI**, 94–8.

Woods, A. (1904b), Co-education up to the age of twelve, *Child Life*, **VI**(24), 181–4.

Woods, A. (1906), In defence of co-education, *Child Life*, **VIII** (29), 8–11.

Woods, A. (1919), (ed.) *Advance in co-education*, Sidgwick and Jackson.

Woods, A. (1925), Co-education in the home, *New Ideals Quarterly* **3** (5), 156–65.

Woods, A. (1931), Questions concerning co-education, *New Ideals Quarterly* **5** (1), 20–2.